THE COMPLETE
# STEP-BY-STEP
# CRAFT BOOK

# THE COMPLETE
# STEP-BY-STEP
# CRAFT
# BOOK

## MORE THAN 450 CREATIVE IDEAS FOR GIFTS AND FOR THE HOME

Whitecap Books

Vancouver / Toronto

This edition published by Whitecap Books Limited
351 Lynn Avenue
North Vancouver
British Columbia
V7J 2C4

1 3 5 7 9 8 6 4 2

ISBN 1 55110 913 1

All correspondence concerning the content of this volume should be
addressed to Salamander Books Ltd.

CREDITS
Project managed by: Charlotte Davies
Designer: John Heritage
Introduction by: Amanda O'Neill
Typeset by: SX Composing DTP
Printed in Spain

# CONTENTS

In recent years, the growing interest in crafts has seen more and more people trying their hands at new craft-based hobbies. In response to the increased demand for craft materials that this has created, manufacturers have developed an increasingly wide range of products and materials. As a result, decorative crafts such as fabric painting or stenciling, which used to require a high degree of technical skill and a great deal of expensive equipment, are now much more accessible and attractive to the general public, thanks to the vast new range of colorful, easy-to-use products.

One of the great delights of craft work is that it enables you to create your own unique style in the home rather than having to conform to a prevalent trend, as you do when buying manufactured designs. You can introduce your personal touch everywhere. Inventive painting techniques such as ragging, sponging, or stenciling transform plain walls; fabric paints can convert soft furnishings, from drapes to pillows, into

**Below:** *A sumptuous design such as this does not have to be expensive; it owes more to a can of gold spray paint and a little ingenuity than to large amounts of money.*

artistic creations. With a paintbrush and a little imagination, you can have new lamps for old – in fact, you can give a new lease of life to old pieces of furniture and uninspired household objects of every kind.

Craft work also comes into its own in the festive season. A handmade gift will always have a more personal touch than a bought one – and you can take matters a stage further by creating your own unique giftwrap and greeting cards. Party time takes on a special air when guests find not just a delightful meal on the table but an individual look created by a decorative centerpiece, personalized placemats, lovingly folded napkins, or a little gift by each plate. You can produce stunning effects at a low cost, and in the colors and styles to suit your décor.

Let's start by looking at the materials and equipment you will need. Some items you will have around already. Old newspapers, empty cartons and cereal packages, boring old plates, or an unloved and uninspiring kitchen chair are all materials for exciting craftwork. Most households will also have some form of drawing kit, scissors, brushes, and so forth, although you may need to extend your collection. For certain projects, such as fabric painting, you

will need to go out and buy the specialist kit required: everything in this book is readily available from artists' suppliers and craft storess.

## Choosing Paints

One of the joys of modern craftwork is the vast range of paints now readily available from craft stores and good department stores. Although, on the whole, the various products are intended for use on specific surfaces, you will find that some paints work well on more than one surface: for example, ceramic paints are suitable for use on glass, metal, and wood, as well as on china.

Glass paints are solvent-based paints which give a stained glass effect on glass, or a translucent finish on china and pottery. They are thick and sticky, so they require some practice to apply correctly. They should always be used and left to dry (for at least 24 hours) in a relatively dust-free environment. The item to be decorated must be totally free from grease or dust before you begin. If necessary, wash the surface with warm, soapy water, rinse and dry it; then wipe it with a cloth soaked in rubbing alcohol or methylated spirits. Apply the paint with a good-quality, soft, clean sable brush, well loaded with

paint. A second coat may be necessary once the first has dried, to achieve a strong enough color. These paints are best reserved for purely decorative items, as they are not intended to stand up to heavy wear and tear.

Ceramic paints are solvent-based paints designed for use on clay and pottery, though they are also suitable for glass, metal, and wood. They need at least 24 hours to dry, and give a glossy, opaque finish. A final coat of ceramic varnish will protect the design to some extent, but these paints will not stand up to much wear and are best reserved for decorative items. Avoid using cutlery on painted plates as this will scratch the surface. Never put decorated objects in a dishwasher; always wash them by hand in warm, soapy water.

Acrylic paints are ideal for painting small wooden objects. They are easier to use than the oil-based gloss paints usually used for larger wooden objects such as doors and baseboards. They come in a wide range of bright colors, and dry very fast to give a rich glossy

**Below:** *Choose from the wide range of craft paints now available. You will also require artists' brushes, a craft knife, masking tape, acetate, masking peel, a sponge, and varnish.*

finish. Unlike gloss paints, they do not require the surface to be prepared with primer and undercoat beforehand: they can be painted straight onto bare wood. They are fully waterproof and are suitable for use both indoors and outdoors. They can also be used for painting designs on walls. One word of warning, though: be sure to clean your brush in water immediately after use – otherwise, the paint will soon dry hard and ruin the brush.

Fabric paints come in various kinds. Most need to be used on unbleached white or naturally colored fabrics for the colors to remain true. However, there are also paints available which are suitable for use on dark fabrics – these "opaque" paints sit on top of the fabric as opposed to being absorbed into it. Fabric felt-tip marker pens are very easy to use, but always remember to tape the fabric down before you begin, to prevent it moving around. Transfer paints are for use on synthetic fabrics, though natural fabrics can be used if they are specially treated first. Silk paints can be used on wool as well as silk. Start by stretching the fabric across a silk or batik frame, available from craft stores. Use special silk pins to attach it. Then you can draw your design on the silk in gutta, a gum-like substance which comes in a special applicator bottle. You have a choice between clear gutta, which is removed when the design is complete, or colored gutta, which outlines each color in the design in the same way that lead outlines stained glass. Be sure to make the lines continuous – any gaps will let the color seep through. Leave the gutta to dry for one hour before painting.

Once a design has been completed, fabric paints must be "fixed" so that the colors do not run when the fabric is washed. Manufacturers will recommend the method best suited for fixing their products, which may include heat or chemical treatments.

For stencil work, manufacturers produce quick-drying, water-based stencil paints and oil-based wax stencil crayons in a wide range of colors. The paints are very economical, and you can use them sparingly to create a subtle cloudy effect or to build up layers, making it possible to stencil a pale color over a dark background. They are also intermixable, so you can make virtually any color you need. The crayons are ideal for a beginner to use, as there is no danger of runny paint leaking under a stencil. The colors blend beautifully and can be quite subtle or bold.

Many paints not made specifically for stenciling can also be used in this way, including fabric and ceramic paints. Regular household water-based paints are ideal for large, simple designs and can be applied with a sponge. Artists' acrylic paints are good for stenciling flexible surfaces such as roller blinds and shower curtains. Cellulose car spray paints can be used on a wide range of surfaces including walls, floors, plastics, and fabrics. They are very durable and you can blend the colors as you are stenciling, but you must mask around the stencil carefully to avoid overspray. Household spray paints are similar and offer further options of pastel shades, such as pink, and peach.

For papier mâché shapes, emulsion (generally white) is the best choice to prime the surface before decoration. Without this, the colors tend to sink into the paper. Alternatively, you can use ready-prepared gesso, obtainable from artists' suppliers. This is more expensive, but it provides a thicker layer and has an attractive, soft appearance. Once the surface is primed, you can use a wide range of paints and colors. Many of the papier mâché projects in this book are finished with gouache colors, while others are painted with household paints – gloss or emulsion. You can also use artist's watercolors, children's chalks, felt-tip marker pens, acrylics, and artists' inks to good effect.

Other coloring products suitable for decorative painting techniques include multi-purpose felt-tip paint pens, designed for a range of surfaces – china, glass, wood, leather, plastic, etc. The pens are easy to use, fast-drying, and available in a wide range of colors. They are solvent-based and their strong smell can prove slightly overpowering, so you are advised to use them in a well-ventilated room.

Finally, to finish off your decorative paintwork, you may require a coat of varnish to protect the surface. Polyurethane varnish is ideal for wood and comes in a matt or gloss finish. Ceramic varnish is specially designed for use on china and pottery. Patina varnish is used to build up a high gloss, lacquer-effect finish on wood. Crackle varnish is applied over patina varnish that is not quite dry, so that the difference in drying rates between the two varnishes causes the crackle varnish to craze, giving an "antique" effect. For papier mâché, acrylic varnish is ideal since it is very clear, but it does make gouache colors run, so it is best to use polyurethane, matt or gloss, over these. If the slightly yellowing effect of polyurethane varnish would spoil the look of the piece, you can obtain clear varnish, designed for use with watercolors and gouache paints, from artists' suppliers.

**Creating Stencils**

You can buy stencils, or make your own. Virtually anything which masks out an area of background will serve as a stencil – a pattern of masking tape, lace, paper doilies, or even something with an interesting outline, such as a leaf. In general, however, the usual stencil is cut out from cardboard or plastic film.

Stencil card is a brown, flexible, oiled cardboard which is very easy to cut, but opaque. This means you have to transfer the design directly onto it and that you cannot see through it to match up the patterns when stenciling. It is inexpensive, but becoming increasingly hard to find as it has been superseded by modern plastic materials. It does not last very long when used with water-based paints, but is excellent for sprayed designs.

Plastic film is usually referred to as acetate, but its correct name is Mylar ®. You can buy it in sheets ready printed with guidelines, especially for stenciling. If you are going to do a lot of stencil cutting, it is more economical to buy large sheets or rolls of special film sold for use in drawing offices. All these plastic films are transparent, which means you can lay the film over a drawn design and cut straight through. You can also see through when stenciling, which is particularly helpful

**Below:** *To change the color scheme of an existing stencil, don't bother making a new one. Mask off the unwanted areas of the old stencil to convert bluebirds into robins!*

**Above:** *Always use a "spray booth" when spraying glue or paint. It is easy to set up by placing a cardboard box on its side. Choose "ozone-friendly" spray glue or paints.*

**Above:** *In addition to the range of papers available in craft shops, consider too using giftwrap or wallpaper for your designs. Ribbons add a finishing touch.*

when lining up a set of stencil patterns.

## Adhesives and Tapes

It is important to use the right glue for the job. Read the manufacturer's directions carefully and test glues on scraps of paper first. When sticking thin papers together, make sure the glue does not seep through the paper. Also take care with printed papers as some glues will smudge the pattern. Use a plastic spreader or strip of cardboard to apply glue evenly over a flat surface.

For a professional finish use spray adhesive. Either put your work on newspaper spread over the work surface or place it inside a box to protect the surrounding area from spray. Spray an even film over the surface and then stick in place. The sprayed paper can be repositioned which is very useful, and any tacky areas can be cleaned up with lighter fuel. Always use an ozone-friendly spray adhesive and work in a well-ventilated room.

PVA (polyvinyl acetate) medium, also known as white glue, has many

purposes. It is a nontoxic, white solution that does not stain, and is quite suitable for children to use. It can be used as a glue and to make papier mâché. As it dries to a clear, glossy finish, it is also useful as a protective varnish.

For papier mâché, wallpaper paste is used to paste the layers of paper pieces. Most brands contain fungicide, and are therefore unsuitable for use by smaller children. Nontoxic paste powder can be obtained from craft stores and educational suppliers. To strengthen the mixture, you can add a little white glue.

Double-sided tape is sticky on both sides and provides a neater, cleaner alternative to glue. Clear sticky tape is very functional but remember that it does yellow and become brittle with age. An alternative is an opaque tape sometimes called magic or invisible tape, which is longer-lasting but does not adhere so well.

Masking tape is a low-tack tape which is handy for holding paper and cardboard in place while you are working, and it does not leave a mark. It is ideal for stencil work, to attach your stencils to the wall without damaging the surface, to mask areas of

the stencil quickly and easily, and to repair any stencils which are torn or cut. It is also useful in papier mâché work, to hold pieces together while glue dries. However where tape is intended to form part of the finished construction – attaching pieces of cardboard, or neatening edges – brown paper tape is recommended.

## Paper and Cardboard

Many of the projects in this book require paper or cardboard. If you look around your home you may be surprised to find how many suitable materials you already have from which to make your designs – from left-over giftwrap and wallpaper to cardboard packages and boxes which can be cut up and re-used. Even old newspapers can be pressed to use for papier mâché objects. You will find that different papers give varying degrees of success, but in general broadsheet papers are of better quality than tabloids.

Artists' suppliers and craft stores stock an inspiring range of special papers. Apart from plain colored papers, there is a wide variety of handmade papers and exotic giftwraps which will add a touch of sophistication to any design. Textured and flock papers are

also available to add a third dimension to collages. Crepe paper is very adaptable because of its stretchy quality, and comes in a wide range of colors. When cut against the grain, the cut edge can be gently stretched to give an attractive fluted edge. Tissue paper and iridescent film, although delicate, can be used to stunning effect on mobiles or as a lining for handmade boxes and bowls. Paper doilies and pictures cut out from greeting cards or magazines are perfect for making gift tags and greeting cards or for decorating boxes.

Brightly colored gummed paper squares are easy to apply – you simply moisten the back and stick them in position. This type of paper is particularly convenient when working on an intricate design.

Generally, where cardboard is required for a project, you should use thin, lightweight cardboard, roughly the same thickness as that used for cereal packages. Where thick cardboard has been suggested, it should be sturdy enough to crease when bent. Some cardboards have a thin coating on one side which has an attractive shiny, metallic, or textured finish. These are particularly good for making party hats and masks. Mounting board can be used for items that will be handled a lot. It is composed of layers of cardboard and comes in a selection of thicknesses.

## Brushes and Tools

For decorative painting, use good quality paintbrushes, and always clean them immediately after use. Brushes used with solvent-based paints should be cleaned in mineral spirit or turpentine substitute; those used with water-based paints should be washed in water.

Specially made stencil brushes are available in different sizes. They can be supplemented with real sea sponges to create a sponged texture on walls before stenciling. Small pieces of the same can be used to create a mottled texture on larger stencils.

A sharp, pointed pair of scissors is essential for working with paper. A small pair is more useful and easier to handle than a large pair. For cutting thick cardboard, and for cutting stencils, you will need a sharp craft knife with replaceable blades, or a scalpel available from craft stores. Always cut on a cutting mat. A purpose-made, rubberized, self-healing cutting mat is the perfect base to draw on. It has a printed grid which is very helpful for drawing accurate guidelines and register marks, and has a non-slip surface. Cutting mats are, however, rather expensive, and a sheet of thick cardboard makes a good substitute in most circumstances. When cutting through thick card, do not try to cut right through in one go but make several cuts, going deeper each time, for a clean line. Cut straight lines against a steel rule, preferably a safety one to protect your fingers.

When cardboard just needs to be folded, first score the surface lightly with a craft knife, making sure not to cut too deep.

A hole punch is useful for making decorative holes, for punching out rounds from colored paper to be glued onto a card, or for making holes in gift tags, through which ribbon can be threaded and attached to parcels. A pair of dividers or a stout needle is useful to make holes in card to sew on buttons, etc. Tweezers are highly recommended for keeping hold of small items when applying glue.

When selecting pencils and drawing aids, you will find a medium hard pencil the most versatile, but a softer lead is better for sketching. Always keep pencils sharpened to a fine point so that your drawing is accurate. Be sure to use a ruler for drawing straight lines, and a set square for drawing squares and rectangles so that the angles are correct. Draw circles with a compass or, for tiny circles, use a plastic stencil. A fine, waterproof felt-tip pen is ideal for drawing thin, accurate guidelines.

## Modeling Material

For a few projects, modeling clay is used to mold small forms. Fimo modeling clay can be molded and cut into the desired shape, then baked in an oven for a few minutes to harden, following the manufacturer's directions. A small rolling pin and board are useful for rolling out the clay, and a spatula can be used for lifting flat shapes from the board.

**Below:** *Look out for unusual materials. Toy shops, notion departments, or tag sales may be a source of decorative trimmings to brighten your designs.*

**Left:** *Old china plates, ceramic tiles, books, magazines, postcards, fabrics, and attractive packaging can all prove a source of inspiration for designs.*

## Trimmings and Ribbons

It is often the finishing touches that make a handmade item so special, and you will find craft stores are a treasure trove of suitable decorative objects – many of them very fairly priced. Cotton pulp or polystyrene shapes are lightweight and suitable for decorating in many ways. Similarly, colored pipecleaners, tiny pompons, stick-on eyes, beads, sequins, and jewelry components all add interest to a design.

Doll's house specialists are invaluable for finding tiny accessories, and stationers can supply an exciting range of attractive stickers and transfers.

Nowadays, there is an exciting range of Victorian scraps that are ideal for paper crafts, plus a wide variety of decorative sticky tapes that help give a professional finish to a project.

Ribbons have many uses, and come in a great many widths and colors, including floral, plaid and printed themes. Ribbon can be curled over scissors, woven, plaited, and glued. Giftwrapping ribbons can also be used to great effect. The wide ones can be moistened so that they will stick to themselves, and the narrow ribbons will coil attractively when pulled smoothly over the blade of a pair of scissors. Braid is another very useful and more unusual material and again is available in a variety of forms and colors.

Flowers are ever-popular motifs, and you can achieve quite different effects by using different sorts – dried, fabric, ribbon, etc. Paper doilies come in a whole range of sizes and patterns and can also be used to striking effect.

## Sources of Inspiration

To begin with, you will probably want to follow the designs featured in this book. But as you become more confident and adventurous, you will find inspiration from a wide range of sources. Old china plates, ceramic tiles, books, magazines, postcards, fabrics, and attractive packaging can all spark off ideas for creating designs of your own. Visits to museums, craft stores, and notion departments can all provide themes, motifs, and jumping-off points or new ideas. Special occasions such as weddings, christenings, or birthday parties all provide their own inspirations.

What to decorate? The possibilities are endless. Thrift stores and charity stores are an inexpensive source of plain plates, boxes, lampshades, and shabby old furniture which cry out to be metamorphosed with an imaginative new paint finish. Specialist craft suppliers stock plain wooden items specially designed for decorating. Or you can always start right from scratch and create your own unique objects in papier mâché.

## How to Make Cards and Stencils

**Above:** *Decide on the size of the card and multiply the width measurement by three. Draw out on a piece of chosen card. Mark the fold lines. Measure the piece of work for mounting and cut a window to fit. Score the two fold marks on the right side of the card. Cut off a ⅛ inch (3mm) strip from the left side.*

**Above:** *Choose a design to suit your requirements from a piece of fabric, wallpaper, giftwrap, a book, or magazine. Use a pencil to carefully trace the shape onto tracing paper. Now convert the motif into a stencil by redrawing it with "bridges," so that whole area of the design is enclosed within a continuous line.*

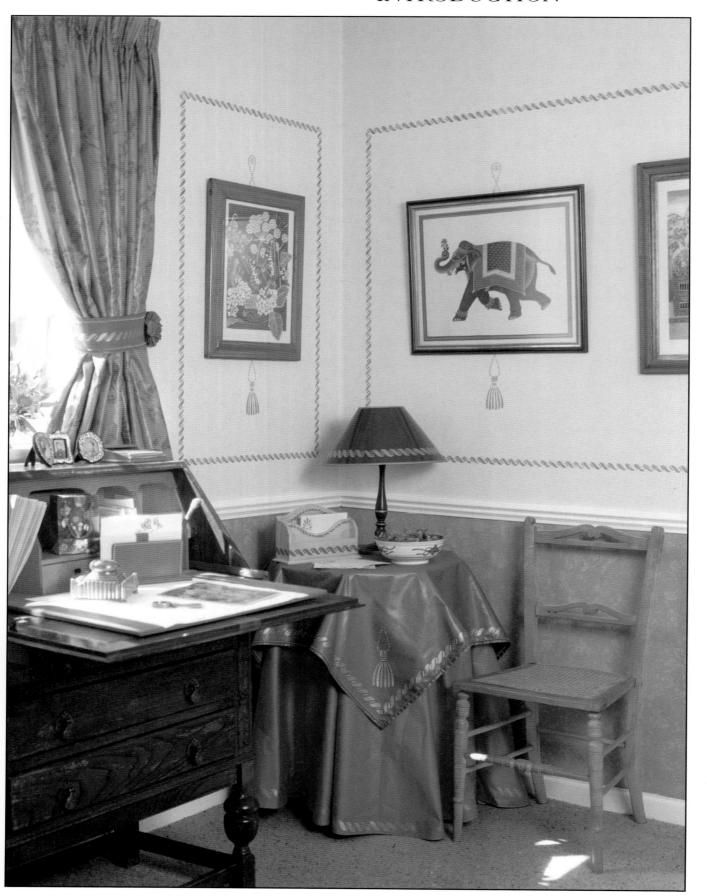

Choose two or three warm colors and subtle textures to create a rich, elegant mood in a small room. Decorate with simple stencils to prevent the designs becoming too distracting. Accentuate pictures with a two-color rope border to make an attractive "frame." Simple accessories can complement the whole theme with touches of the rope border in the same shades or with gold and copper luster to add sparkle. Select stencils from the Template Section (page 243) to transform any room in your home.

*Experiment with stencil designs in a range of colors and situations to change the mood and style of any room. In this study the stenciled wall decorations and soft furnishing accessories bring an air of simple elegance to the once-plain surroundings.*

If the present you have bought is an awkward shape, don't waste time trying to wrap it neatly. Instead, make a box or a bag and put the present inside. With the minimum of fuss and effort you can create an attractively presented gift and the person who receives your present enjoys the added bonus of being able to use the box or bag again afterwards.

In the Gift Wrapping chapter you will find instructions for making an assortment of cardboard boxes. The templates for these boxes can be found on pages 252–253 and by scaling them up or down you can make a box in any size you like.

*Why not try your hand at making an original container from this varied selection of gift boxes and bags. They are completely professional in finish, yet remarkably straightforward to make and will suit presents of any size or shape.*

Usually it is easy to guess the contents of a gift if the gift is a recognizable shape – but not if you disguise it. Throughout this book you will find ideas and inspiration for turning a bottle into a pencil for example, a record into a pillow, a cube into a dice, or even a circular gift into a hat.

Many of the gift-wrapping ideas in this book can be used at any time but there are also a number of projects especially devised for celebrating special occasions. Wrapping gifts for Christmas, Easter, weddings, christenings, or Valentine's Day usually requires extra inspiration. There are plenty of exciting designs to choose from to bring a touch of originality.

*Whether your present is for Christmas, Valentine's Day, or a christening, you can have great fun wrapping it to match the occasion. You can even disguise it as a birthday cake or a domino. No one will ever guess what is inside.*

The huge selection of giftwraps now available from a range of outlets should give you plenty of scope for covering your gifts. You don't have to use store-bought giftwrap however – for a more stylish, individual touch you can easily make your own. There are plenty of ideas to choose from in the pages that follow. For example, what about stenciling your own design, creating a collage, or printing a pattern with a humble potato?

And once you have your giftwrap, there are plenty of useful tips on how to use it most effectively, such as wrapping a cylindrical gift neatly, or what to do with a spherical shape.

*There's no excuse for an unimaginatively wrapped present with such a spectacular range of giftwrap available. Choose from plain, matt, shiny, pastel or bold colours, glossy or glittery designs, to make the most of your gift.*

# INTRODUCTION

To ensure that your greeting cards have a professional finish, you must select the correct weight of card - not too thin so that it curls or fall over, or too thick. To make a neat fold in card, score on the right side with a light cut using a sharp craft knife and a steel ruler, just piercing the top layer of card. The card will then fold in a straight line. Unless otherwise stated, all the cards in the chapter on Greeting Cards are folded vertically. Always measure carefully and mark with a sharp pencil to create a fine line. Should your finished card be crooked, trim a new straight edge using a set square and with the card folded so that you can cut through back and front thicknesses at once. Draw the blade twice along the cutting edge.

*Card comes in a variety of finishes, cloud effect, metallic, parchment style, textured, glossy and matt. Tissue, brown paper, origami, marbled, wall and wrapping paper, foil and plastic bags can all be used to create different effects.*

# INTRODUCTION

The decorative details on a gift can make all the difference to the finished article. The wrapping paper might be bright and attractive, but if the present is lacking decoration it can still look dull. Even a pretty bow can provide the finishing touch you need to turn a plain parcel into a chic gift.

Buying manufactured ribbon pom-poms to match your paper can make gift wrapping highly expensive. In the chapter on Gift Wrapping you will find instructions on how to make all sorts of ribbon decorations for yourself that look just as good as the shop-bought kinds. You can also create your own tassels, foil stars, paper ruffles, and flowers of all kinds.

*Reels of gift ribbon can be turned into an array of different decorations, from stunning rosettes to individual and original pom-poms. Braid, cord, tissues and even sweets can be used to decorate your gifts and make parcels look extra-special.*

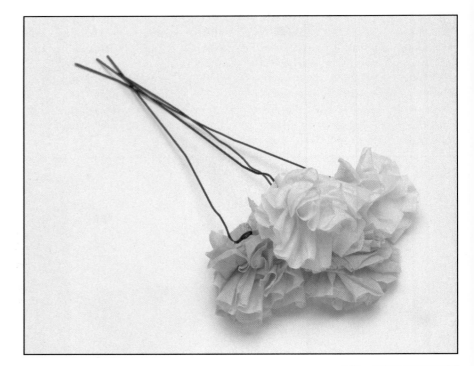

This is something we probably all learned at school but many of us have long forgotten! First you need to choose a bowl or some other receptacle that is roughly the shape you wish to achieve. Tear up lots of newspaper into narrow strips. Then make up a flour and water paste, not too stiff, not too runny. You will soon discover the correct consistency when you get started.

Dip the newspaper into the paste and start placing it on the bowl, working your way around it until the whole surface is covered. Keep working over it, in all directions, until you have built up at least six layers. This will give you a firm mold. Make sure to keep it smooth as you go along.

When you have finished, leave the papier-mâché to dry in a warm, dry place. It will take about 24 hours to dry completely – more if it is particularly thick. When it is ready, ease it off the bowl. You may have to sand down the rough edges, but this is best done after the first coat of paint, as this will show up any lumps and bumps.

These little carnation-shaped flowers are useful for adorning all sorts of decorations, or can be used by themselves to make a lovely floral centerpiece. Take a regular paper tissue and cut it in half lengthwise. Concertina-fold it down its length, as shown, then tie it in the middle with a piece of wire or twine.

Fold the tissue in half, and wrap one end of the wire firmly around the base to hold the shape in position. (The other end serves as the stem.)

Now simply fluff out the paper, teasing it with your fingers until it resembles a carnation.

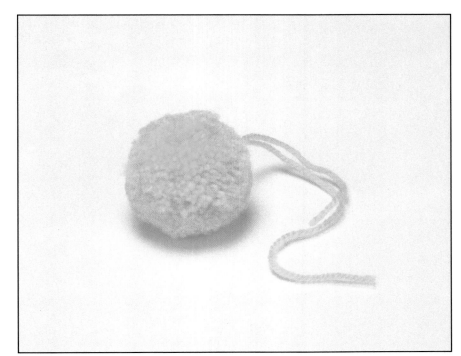

Tassels are useful for trimming hats or the edges of hanging decorations, and they are very easy to make. Cut several strands of yarn or cord; the more you cut, the fuller the tassel will be. The strands should be twice the finished length of the tassel. Tie them firmly in the center. Leave the tying strands uncut, and fold the tassel strands in half.

Now wind a cord several times around all the strands, about 1 inch (2.5cm) from the top (or less, for a small tassel). Tie it firmly and cut off the ends.

Trim the ends off the tassel so that they are all the same length. Use the top cord to attach it to whatever you are trimming.

These jolly trimmings, ideal for party hats, can be made of yarn left over from knitting projects. First cut two rounds of cardboard with a diameter the size you wish the finished pompon to be. Cut a fairly large hole in the center. Now wind yarn (doubled, to speed up the work) over the cardboard rings until you can barely push the yarn through any more.

The more yarn you use, the bushier the pompon will be. Cut a fairly large hole in the center. Now wind yarn (doubled, to speed up the work) over the cardboard rings until you can barely push the yarn through any more.

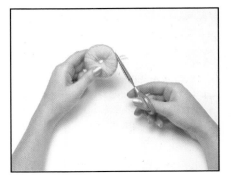

Wind a piece of yarn between the cardboard rings around all the strands. Pull firmly and make a strong knot, leaving long ends. Now take out the rings. Finish by trimming off any straggling ends of yarn.

# FOR THE HOME

Sponging is one of the easiest paint finishes to achieve. You can use one, two, or more colors. When choosing colors, go for a light, mid, and darker shade of the same color. Here, rose white has been used as a base for soft peach and dusky apricot. It is a good idea to buy some small samples of water-based paint to practice with before you start. First, apply the base coat with a brush or roller.

When your base color is dry, take a natural sponge and dampen it. Now dip the sponge into the second color, being careful not to overload it with paint. Remove any excess paint by dabbing the sponge onto waste paper, then apply paint to the walls with a light dabbing motion. Don't press hard or the paint will smudge. Continue in a random pattern, reapplying paint to the sponge as necessary.

Wash out your sponge and apply the third color, overlapping the second color. When you have finished, you should have an even blending of the three colors. If the last color is too dominant, you can soften it by sponging over with some of the base color.

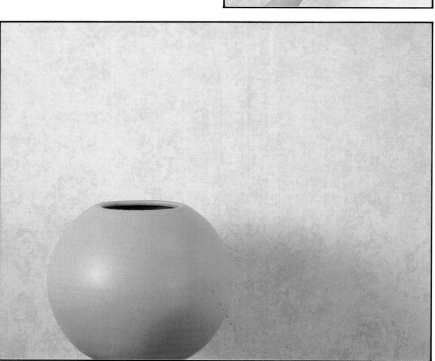

There are two main methods of ragging: "ragging off," in which you apply rags to a wet wall of paint, so removing the color and leaving a pattern; or "ragging on" as shown here. In the latter, the color is applied with bunched-up rags, in a similar way to sponging. First apply a base coat of water-based paint with a roller or a brush.

Use dry rags for this technique – it is the crisp folds in the fabric that form the pattern. Make sure you cut up lots of rags before you start and have plenty of waste paper around. Clasp a rag in your hand and dip it lightly into the paint. Dab off the top layer of paint onto some waste paper, then apply the cloth to the wall with a dabbing motion.

Continue to apply paint in a random pattern, replacing the rag with a fresh one as soon as it becomes too damp. When the first color has dried, apply a second color as before: a contrasting color can look particularly effective.

# FREE-HAND FLORAL TILES

A very easy way of painting tiles is to use multi-purpose felt-tip paint pens. Assuming each square represents one tile, square up your design and transfer it onto the tiles using a Chinagraph pencil. Draw over this line with a fine line felt-tip paint pen. Try to keep the paint flowing once you have put the pen onto the tile so that the line is continuous.

Color in your design using both thick and fine line pens. Be as outrageous as you like with your use of colors, placing reds, oranges, and pinks together, and adding a sparkle with gold and silver.

Add to the range of tones and colors with plenty of dots and lines in contrasting colors. To finish, protect your design with a coat of ceramic varnish once the paints are dry.

# MARVELOUS MARBLING

This must be the easiest way of achieving a stylish effect. All you need are some plain white tiles, ceramic or glass paints, mineral spirit, a large bowl full of water, a small mixing bowl or saucer, and a paint brush. You may also wish to wear rubber gloves to protect your hands. Thin some paint with mineral spirits and begin to drop it onto the surface of the water with a paint brush.

Using the handle of the paint brush or an old stick, mix the color round so that it creates a swirling pattern. If you wish, you can dilute a second color in the same way and add this to the first.

Carefully hold the glazed side of the tile against the surface of the water and then quickly lift it away. The tile will pick up the swirls of paint to give a marbled effect. Leave the tile to dry, then give it a coat or ceramic varnish to protect the finish. You may find it necessary to practice this technique for a while before you perfect it.

These attractive full-length drapes will add style to any modern living-room and can be painted in any color to match the décor. You will need lots of space when painting the fabric so cover your floor with plenty of newspaper before you begin. Now rip sheets and sheets of newspaper into long strips. It is best to use broadsheet newspapers as they are wider and have more pages.

Sew together enough fabric to make a drape and lay it out on the floor. Tape several strips of newspaper together so that they fit across the width of your fabric. Now, using loops of masking tape on the underside of the paper, stick the strips to the cloth, leaving gaps between the rows. As you work your way toward the top of the cloth, break up the rows with small "islands" of paper.

Pour some opaque black fabric paint onto a saucer or plate. Starting at the bottom of the cloth, sponge the paint between the rows of newspaper.

With each new row, mix a little white opaque fabric paint into the black before you dip the sponge in. Keep adding white with each successive row so that the color gradually changes from black to gray as you print up the cloth. By the time you get to the top where you have the islands of paper, the color should be light gray.

Leave the fabric paint to dry before removing the paper. Repeat the whole procedure with the second drape. Iron on the back of each piece of fabric to fix the color and then make them up into drapes.

This is a very simple but effective design for a shade. All you need is a plain shade, some chalk, black fabric paint, a black fabric felt-tip pen, and your own foot! Draw round your foot on tracing paper and cut out the shape. Use this as a template to draw feet onto the shade with chalk, drawing the toes individually as shown. Keep turning the template over to get left and right footprints.

When you have chalked your design, going up and down the shade, draw over the chalk with a black fabric pen. Fill in the center of each foot with black fabric paint, then iron on the reverse side of the fabric to fix the color.

Forget city life and make-believe you live in a home by the sea with this colorful shade. A photograph of a sea gull is a useful reference when drawing the bird. Create your design at a reasonable size first, then square it up to full size so that it fits on the shade. Draw the design onto a plain white shade in pencil.

When painting such a complex picture, it is a good idea to paint the background first, so start with the sky. This is a mixture of white and blue fabric paint, sponged on quite densely. The clouds are sponged on more lightly. Once the background is painted, start painting in the details. When you've finished, iron the back of the fabric to fix the paints.

Here's something for those who enjoy the outrageous and the avant garde – an old standing lamp eye-catchingly decorated with Doric columns and oak leaves. Following the maker's directions, strip the original finish off the standing lamp with varnish remover. Use an old toothbrush to get into difficult corners. Rub down the surface with wire wool, then sand it to give a smooth finish.

Paint the lamp with primer and, when this is dry, apply some undercoat. Alternatively, you could use two coats of combined primer/undercoat. Leave it to dry before you begin to apply the color.

Decorate the lamp stand with acrylic paints, using bold, primary colors. Paint different parts of the stand different colors, and break the colors up with rings of white, using the carved features as guidelines.

Now decorate the base colors with dots, dashes, spots, leaves, and columns, using both acrylic paints and multi-purpose felt-tip paint pens. Paint the spots by sticking ring reinforcements onto one section of the stand and filling in the holes with a brightly contrasting color. Paint black oak leaves on another section and outline them in bright yellow using the felt-tip pens.

When the lamp stand is dry, apply a coat of protective varnish. Outline your design on the shade with a fine line fabric felt-tip pen, repeating the patterns used on the stand. Now fill in the design with thick fabric pens, continuing to use brightly contrasting colors.

Cover the base with black tissue paper, torn into squares of approximately 4 inches (10cm). Paint one side of the paper and apply this side to the lamp, overlapping pieces slightly. Give the feet three coats of poster paint, and then paint the entire base with matt polyurethane varnish. Finish with fire retardant, available from theatrical suppliers.

Using a craft knife, make two more holes in the base – one at the top for the light fitting, and one about 1 inch (2.5cm) away from the hole at the bottom, to carry the cord. When you wire the lamp, fit a cord grip inside the lamp to secure the cord.

For the shade, it is simplest to use an existing shade to make the pattern. Mark the outline on thin paper, such as newspaper. Cut this out and place over the existing shade to check for fit. When you are satisfied, mark the outlines on thin cardboard or thick cartridge paper, making sure that there is a sufficient crossover.

A cheap plastic beach ball, approximately 14 inches (35cm) in diameter, is used for the base. Coat it with petroleum jelly and then apply six layers of papier mâché all over, using pieces about 3 inches (7.5cm) square. When the last layer has dried, mark a line around the shape and carefully cut with a craft knife. Then remove the papier mâché.

Tear tissue paper into 4-inch (10cm) squares and apply it to the cardboard – the pencil outlines will still be visible through the paper. Pink tissue paper was used first, and these were overlaid with strips of blue and yellow, to create purple and orange tones. Cut out the shade and hold it over a lighted lamp – add more pieces if needed (we added some black).

Glue the edges and hold them with masking tape until set. Then remove the tape and cover the join with two layers of papier mâché. Using a small bowl, mark a circle, large enough for your hand to fit through, on the ball shape and cut it out. Make three large balls. When dry, slice a small section from each, so that they can lie flat. Attach the feet around the hole with epoxy glue.

Paint the overlapping edges with white glue; hold with masking tape until dry. Using new supports or those from the old shade, attach them with white glue, having first given them a coat of white water-based paint. Treat the finished shade with fire retardant, available from theatrical suppliers.

A plain lampshade is decorated with a simple ivy motif, colored in with pearlized fabric paints. First, draw the design onto tracing paper, then pencil over the shapes on the reverse side. Tape the trace in position over the shade and transfer the design by following the outline once more.

Go over the motif in pencil to make the images stronger. When this is done, you can color in the design. If you cannot buy pearlized fabric paint, use opaque fabric paint on dark background colors, or regular fabric paints on light backgrounds. When the design is complete, fix the color by holding the shade under a hot hair drier for a few minutes.

The inspiration for this lamp came from a small evening bag. Either copy the design used here or find an alternative source of inspiration, such as a piece of fabric, a greeting card, or a porcelain plate. Then experiment with the colors you are going to use, coloring in the design with felt-tip pens.

Trace your design onto the shade and color it in using brightly colored fabric felt-tip pens. Edge the motifs in stronger color. Now paint the design onto the lamp base using ceramic paints. If you do not feel confident about painting the shapes straight onto the surface, draw them on first with a Chinagraph pencil.

Leave the first color to dry before edging the design in a lighter shade. You will need to fix the paint on the lampshade by heating it with a hair drier for a few minutes.

In this colorful design, a wall light is transformed into an umbrella bursting with toys. First mark the segments of the umbrella by putting strips of masking tape onto the shade as shown and ruling down one edge of each strip with a multi-purpose felt-tip paint pen. Remove the tape and color each segment using acrylic paints. Draw an outline of the shade onto the wall.

Draw the various elements of the design in pencil onto tracing paper – restrict your shapes to balloons, balls, and kites if you are not too confident about more complex shapes. Pencil over the reverse of each trace and transfer the images onto the wall. As before, use acrylic paints to color in the toys. Complete the picture by fixing the shade in position.

For those of you who like plants but lack green fingers, why not paint your own plant, cascading down from a wall lamp? Make an outline of your shade onto the wall so you know where to position the plant. Now, using a house plant as reference, draw the design onto the wall. Use a pencil so you can erase any mistakes.

If you are using a translucent lightshade like this one, you can draw some of the leaves within the outline so that they show through the shade. Paint the leaves using acrylic paints or even artists' oils, though the latter will take a little longer to dry. Use dark colors to create shadow and depth, and light colors to add highlights. Finally, fix your shade in place. As you can see, the effect is stunning.

# KITCHEN LAMPSHADE

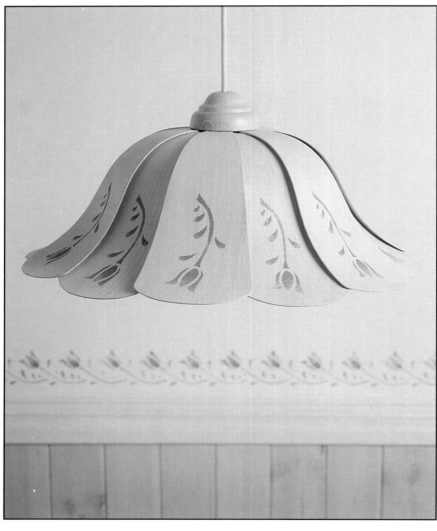

S tencil a pretty pine lampshade to hang over the corner table and complete the setting. Sand the wood smooth and paint with two or three coats of pale blue satin varnish. Use a single flower motif and trim the acetate to fit one section. Place the stencil centrally and draw in the outline of the section to align the stencil accurately each time.

Tape the stencil on one section and stencil all over with quick-drying stencil paint in pale blue. Use a clean brush and lightly shade the base of the flower and leaves with a darker blue–gray paint. Leave to dry and give the whole shade a coat of clear matt varnish to complete it.

Size as required: suggest one square represents ¾ inch (2cm)

An old piece of utility furniture, long past its prime, is transformed with a beautiful paint finish and some new china handles. Choose a light-colored, water-based paint for the base color, plus a medium and a dark shade for the sponging on. Before you can start to redecorate, you will need to remove the old finish.

Place the piece of furniture in a well-ventilated room, standing it on plenty of newspaper to protect the surrounding floor. Apply paint stripper according to the manufacturer's directions. Leave for the required length of time and then scrape off the old paint. Wash down the surface with liquid detergent and water. When dry, sand it until the wood is smooth.

Next, apply a primer, an undercoat, and then a water-based paint base color, leaving the cabinet to dry between coats. Take a natural sponge and wet it, then squeeze it so it is just damp. Dip it into your second color and dab any excess paint onto waste paper before applying paint to the cupboard. Use a light dabbing motion so that you do not smudge the paint, and leave lots of gaps for the next color.

Apply the third and darkest color with a clean sponge, filling in any gaps and overlapping other sponged areas.

Finally, using ceramic paint, decorate some plain white china handles with a pretty leaf or floral pattern. If you need inspiration for your design, try looking at an old china cup or plate.

Using red, green, and blue acrylic paint and a fine paint brush, paint the cross pieces, the central dowels, and the ends of the legs and arms in alternating bright colors. Acrylic paints dry very quickly, so clean your brush instantly between each color.

When the paint is completely dry, give the frame a couple of coats of varnish to protect it. Leave the first coat to dry before applying the second one.

Using either the original covers or some new fabric cut to size, put strips of masking tape across the canvas, masking off a series of rectangles both large and small. Rub the tape down with the back of a spoon to give it extra adhesion.

A striking "Mondrian"-inspired design in bold colors gives a new lease of life to a battered old director's chair. Even if you don't have an old chair to do up, it's still worth buying a new one to customize. As well as paint brushes, masking tape, and a sponge, you will also require varnish, acrylic paints, opaque fabric paints, and a black fabric paint pen.

Pour some opaque fabric paint into a saucer and dip a sponge into the color. Dab the paint onto a masked area of the canvas, being sure not to get any paint on the adjacent squares. Use a sponge rather than a paint brush to avoid brush strokes. When you have finished applying one color, take a clean sponge and apply the next. Continue like this until all the rectangles are filled in.

Remove the canvas from your chair; if it is old, you can replace it later with new deck chair canvas. Sand down the chair frame until the wood is smooth and fill any cracks with wood putty. Now paint the outline of the frame with black acrylic paint, applying a second coat if necessary.

You may find you have to use more than one coat of paint if you are working on a very dark background. When the paint is completely dry, tear off all the masking tape. Finish by drawing a black rule round each of the rectangles, using a fabric paint pen. You can now put the canvas back on the chair.

Here's a cheerful way to decorate some inexpensive plastic chairs for a party or a kid's playroom. All you need are some fine multi-purpose felt-tip pens and a Chinagraph pencil. Using the Chinagraph pencil, draw your design onto the seat and the back of the chair, creating bold shapes and patterns. Erase any mistakes with a soft cloth soaked in lighter fuel.

Color in your outlines with the multi-purpose pens, using brightly contrasting and even clashing colors. Decorate the stars with dots, spots, dashes, and triangles of black.

Outline the edges of the shapes in black to make the images sharper. Finally, link up the various elements of your design with colorful streamers and more dots and dashes.

This chair was inspired by designs of the "Bloomsbury Group" (a London-based group of artists and writers). First, give a plain wooden chair a fresh coat of gloss paint. Then, referring to the pattern in the main photograph, draw the design onto the surface using a fine black felt-tip pen.

Using gloss paints, color in the design with a fine brush, making sure you just cover the black outlines so that the design remains soft, rather than hard-edged.

Bambooing is a simple but effective paint technique which can add interest to a plain piece of cane furniture. Before you start to paint, remove any varnish from your furniture with varnish remover. Dilute some brown acrylic paint with water to make a wash. Then, using a ¾-inch (20-mm) brush, paint bands of color at intervals along the cane.

Next, using the same color undiluted and a fine brush, paint on the markings. First, paint lines of color in the center of the band of wash. Next paint elongated "V" shapes in pairs at right angles to the lines, finishing off with tiny dots by the sides of the Vs. When the bambooing is complete, apply a coat of varnish to protect the paintwork.

In recent years, Lloyd loom chairs such as this have become collectors' items. But because so many of them are now in poor condition, they are often renovated and painted with an attractive motif. The flamboyance of this design is intended to reflect the warm sunny conservatory for which such chairs were originally intended.

You can either paint the chair using aerosol spray paint or apply paint in the traditional manner with a paint brush. Draw your rose design onto the chair, using a soft pencil and keeping the flowers big and bold. Color in the design with acrylic paints, mixing the colors to get a wide range of shades. Use dark shades to add shadow and depth, and lighter shades for the highlights.

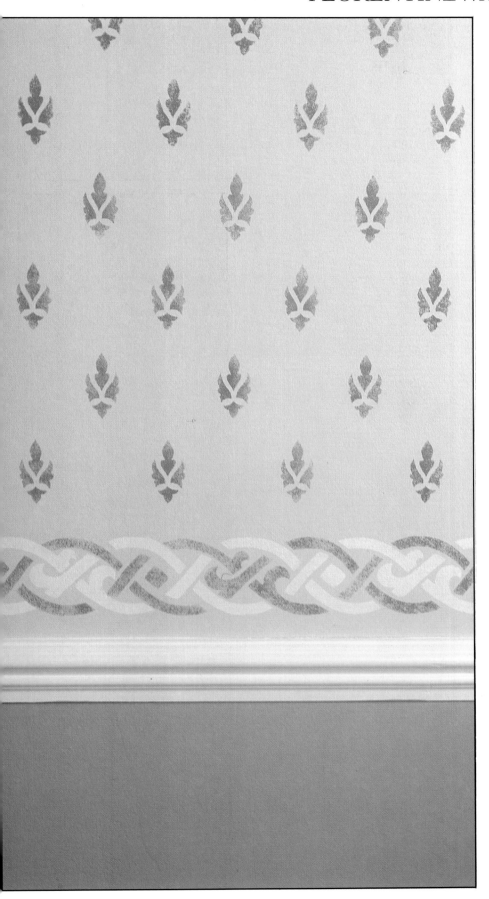

Trace off the Florentine motif from page 247. Draw out the pattern carefully, spacing the motifs evenly about 3½ inches (9cm) apart vertically and 3 inches (7.5cm) apart horizontally. You will need a minimum of two motifs for small areas, but you will greatly speed up the stenciling if you cut a sheet with six or eight motifs. Also draw on vertical guidelines and dotted motif outlines.

Find the center of the wall and use a plumb line to mark a vertical pencil line down to the chair rail. Join up the pencil marks with a long ruler and use this line to begin stenciling.

Start near the top of the wall and work one row of motifs vertically down the plumb line. Make pencil marks first so that the design starts about 2 inches (5cm) from the ceiling and leaves a 4½ inches (11.5cm) space above the chair rail for the border. Mix up some gray quick-drying stencil paint and brush the stencil lightly to give a soft, grainy texture.

When using a small, two-motif stencil, overlap the lower motif you have stenciled with the top one on the acetate sheet to space the first row accurately. The small stencil is useful in tight corners and close to door frames to prevent bending the acetate too much.

Work the next vertical row of motifs, matching up the dotted areas with the first row of stenciling. Continue all over the wall. Adjust the space between rows very slightly to accommodate awkward corners. Stencil within 5 inches (13cm) of the mirror edge. If there are large gaps near the curved area, leave them and add another motif later when the border is complete.

You will need to adapt the original bluebird pattern for this prettily decorated chest of drawers. Trace off the central bow from page 247 and turn the design slightly so that the ribbon tails hang vertically. To balance the bow, sketch in another loop of ribbon on the left. Also use the bow design on page 38.

Trace off the new bow design onto a small piece of acetate using a fine waterproof felt-tip pen. Mark the position of the bird stencils on either side to align the design when stenciling. Cut out the shapes carefully using a sharp craft knife and a cutting mat. Also make a bird stencil. Alternatively, use part of the complete stencil if you have one already made.

If you are only using part of a complete design, mask off the areas of stencil you do not want with paper and masking tape. Mark the center of the drawer with a pencil line. Stencil either side, reversing the stencil as needed. Use quick-drying stencil paint over a base coat of water-based paint Once dry, finish off with a coat of clear varnish.

A painted Lloyd Loom chair is an ideal accessory for this child's bedroom. As the wall stencil is too detailed for the texture of the chair, a bolder version of the design has been chosen. Use the pattern on page 247 to cut three stencils from acetate. Tape the bow stencil centrally on the chair back and mask all around. Spray with household spray paint in soft peach.

Position a bird stencil on the left of the chair beside the bow. Tape in place and mask as before. Spray the bird in white. Spray several thin coats from about 12 inches (30cm) away, until the weave of the chair is well covered but not clogged. Leave to dry, then carefully remove the stencil and mask. Repeat with the other bird stencil to complete the design.

# BLUEBIRD BORDER

F ollow the pattern opposite to make your full-size stencil. Trace off the bluebirds onto a sheet of clear acetate using a fine waterproof felt-tip pen. Also trace off some parts of the peach bows, using a dotted line, to help position the stencil. Mark the top and side lines as register marks, then cut out the bird shapes using a craft knife.

Make another stencil for the bows. Mark a faint horizontal pencil line along the wall to line up with the top register mark on the stencil. Tape the stencil in position and, using soft peach quick-drying stencil paint, stencil the bow design. Keep the paint fairly thin and leave to dry. With a clean brush and terra cotta paint, dab the areas where the ribbon twists to give a 3-D effect.

Using the bluebird stencil, tape the acetate in position, lining up your register marks and matching the dotted lines with the stenciled bows. Carefully dab slate blue stencil paint over the birds. Make sure the whole design is covered, but keep the brush fairly dry to avoid paint seeping underneath. Wipe the surface often to prevent small holes in the stencil becoming clogged.

One square represents 2cm (¾in)

# RIBBON BOWS

One square represents 1cm (½in)

U se this delicate bow to "hang" small pictures in your bluebird bedroom. The ribbons at the side interlock, so you can also use it as a pretty border pattern. Trace off and cut out the design opposite on acetate. Tape the stencil just above the picture so that the ends of the ribbons will disappear behind the frame. Stencil with quick–drying stencil paint in soft peach.

When the paint has dried slightly, use a clean brush to lightly dab on some terracotta color stencil paint. Do this where the ribbons twist and overlap to give a 3-D effect and make the ribbon look almost shiny. Blend the terracotta paint into the soft peach to avoid a sudden color change.

The plain flush doors in this modern hall looked very boring, so to add a little character they have been stenciled with four gray borders to give a paneled look. Start by marking out the panels with pencil lines, using a long ruler and set-square for accuracy. The borders should be about ⅝ inch (1.5cm) wide, with the space at the bottom of the door greater than the top and sides.

Use long strips of masking tape to mask off around the border, on both sides. Press down the tape with a fingertip to prevent paint from seeping underneath and cut the corners neatly with a sharp craft knife. On an old plate, mix up some white, gray and black quick-drying stencil paints. If the door paint is very shiny, lightly sand the border area first to make a key for the stenciling.

If your light source is on the right, start by stenciling the left-hand side of each panel in a medium gray, dabbing the paint on thinly and evenly. Mask the top and bottom corners of this line with tape to form a 45° angle (like the mitered corner of a frame.) (If the light comes from the left, start stenciling on the right-hand side of each panel.)

Leave to dry for a few minutes and remove the angled corner tapes. Then stencil the top and right-hand border in dark gray (top and left-hand border, if light comes from the left.) Mask the corners at an angle, as before. Stencil a thin, even coating of color, getting slightly paler toward the bottom of the panel.

Lastly, stencil the lower border in pale gray as it will theoretically get the most amount of light. Leave to dry and very carefully pull off the masking tape. For economy, these tapes can be used several times. Stencil all the other panels on the door. Then clean off the pencil marks with a damp cloth when the paint has dried.

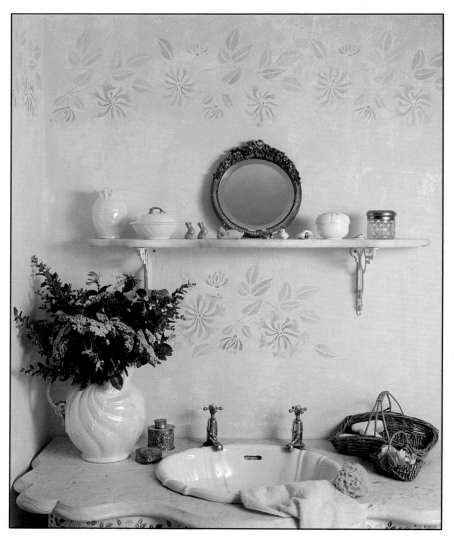

To create this beautiful effect, first paint your walls in white silk vinyl. Then sponge pale, sunny yellow water-based paint over the top to make a warm, cloudy effect. Dip a large, damp natural sponge into a saucer of paint, taking care not to overload the sponge. Dab off the excess onto a spare piece of cardboard, then dab onto the wall in an even pattern.

Enlarge and cut two stencil sheets from the design on page 41. Lightly mark the desired level on the wall and tape the flower stencil in place. Use a small piece of natural sponge and dip it into a saucer containing pale peach or yellow stencil paint or water-based paint. Tester pots are ideal for this purpose. Dab onto the stencil around the edge of each circle of flowers.

Mix up a subtle pinky-orange and sponge-stencil this onto the center of each group of flowers. Gradually blend the pink with the yellow to make a soft orange. Stencil all the flowers around the wall like this, linking the design with the dotted lines on the stencil.

Tape on the leaf stencil and mix a few shades of green from lime to emerald on an old plate. Use another piece of sponge to stencil the leaves and stems. Try to vary the shades of green over the design, to give added interest. Dab lightly for a mottled texture that blends with the wall sponging.

# BATHED IN FLOWERS

One square represents 2 inches (5cm)

Enlarge and cut out two stencils from the honeysuckle design opposite. Clean the outside of the bathtub thoroughly. If necessary you can spray paint before stenciling. Spray glue over the back of the first stencil and tape in place. Mask all around with plenty of waste paper to protect from overspray. Using household spray paint, held about 12 inches (30cm) away, spray the flowers lightly in yellow.

Leave to dry for a few moments. Meanwhile, shake a can of pink spray paint to mix it thoroughly. When the first color is touch-dry, spray the center of each circle of flowers with a burst of pink to shade it subtly.

Tape the leaf stencil in place, lining up the flowers with the dotted lines on the acetate. Tape waste paper all around as before and lightly spray the leaves in green. Add a little extra green in a few places to liven it up. Stencil all around the bathtub, then leave the paint to dry thoroughly before use.

Draw a door plate shape on cardboard (you might draw around an existing plate). Draw a simple squiggle down the middle, as shown. Cut the shape out.

Using sisal, for thickness, glue string around the shape, just inside the edge. Glue thinner package string along the squiggle shape.

Using small pieces to maintain as much definition as possible, papier mâché over the string and on the front and back of the plate. Apply up to four layers.

Give the door plate two coats of water–based paint and then a coat of light green gloss.

When this has dried, sponge on darker green paint. When dry, lay the door plate on a sheet of newspaper and splash red gloss paint over it, creating a "Jackson Pollock" effect. Make a hole at the top and bottom, so that it can be attached to the door.

This decorative column is based on one seen in Savannah, Georgia. Start by drawing the shape, which measures approximately 10 by 21 inches (25 by 53cm) on a drawing board. Roll out a clay sausage about 1 inch (2.5cm) thick, and press it along the line, flattening the base to make the roll D-shaped. Coat the shape and 2 inches (5cm) of board on either side with petroleum jelly.

All at one go, apply four layers of 4 inches (10cm) square papier mâché (you may require smaller pieces on inner curves). The vertical lines are made from lengths of semicircular wooden dowel, sanded into rounds at each end. These are simply given two coats of white water-based paint. When dry, cut the papier mâché from the board and remove the clay. Clean the flat edges with mineral spirit.

Sand and seal the surface, and apply two coats of water-based paint. Draw a line ¼ inch (6mm) out from the raised surface and trim away the excess. Position the pieces on the wall with masking tape and draw around them. Take them down and apply impact adhesive to the column pieces and the wall. Then fix them in place, filling any gaps with ready-mix plaster.

A brightly decorated clock makes a novel gift for a child. Self-assembly clocks like this one are available from some craft suppliers (particularly by mail order), so check in craft magazines for stockists. First, sand down the clock so that it is perfectly smooth, then draw your design in pencil. Use bright acrylic paints to color the design.

When the painting is complete, assemble the clock according to the manufacturer's directions. Apply a coat of polyurethane varnish for a glossy finish.

A vine leaf design is used to enhance a plain mirror frame. The design can be painted with acrylic or a combination of ceramic and glass paints, using different shades of green, plus brown, white, yellow, and black. Protect the glass before you start painting with a layer of paper stuck down around the edges with masking tape.

To age the frame, stain it with brown and green glass paint diluted with turpentine. When the stain is dry, finish with a coat of varnish. Another way of aging the frame is to use the "crackle" varnish method (see page 7.)

Firmly tape all the pieces together around the outer edge. Give the resulting frame four layers of papier mâché and leave it to dry.

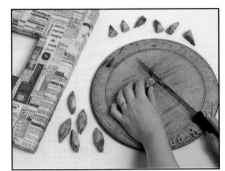

Using a quarter of a broadsheet each time, crumple nine pieces of newspaper and leave them in paste overnight. Squeeze out the excess paste and form them into sausages, pointed at each end. When dry, after several days, cut each in half with a breadknife, making 18 points of slightly varied sizes.

Using epoxy resin glue, fix the points around the frame, spacing them evenly. Work on one edge at a time, supporting the frame so that the edge on which you are working is horizontal. When you have finished, leave the glue to harden before decorating the frame.

Paint the frame with five layers of ready-prepared gesso. Draw the surface lines with a pencil, and then paint lines on the front and the edges with three coats of gold poster paint. When this has dried, apply a coat of matt polyurethane varnish, giving the white a slightly aged quality.

Made with an ordinary mirror tile, this would be ideal for a hallway. Instead of water-based paint, the white ground of the frame has been painted with gesso to add textural interest. Cut eight pieces of cardboard, each measuring 12 by 16 inches (30 by 40cm.) Cut windows from each, as shown in the diagram, discarding all the centers except for the largest.

When the varnish has dried, place a 6 inch (15cm) mirror tile in the back of the frame. You may need to back it with a piece of cardboard the same size. Finally, fix the spare cardboard window over the tile, using epoxy resin glue to hold it in place. Brass eye screws can be used for hanging the frame.

# ORNAMENTAL COLUMN

Cut two more circles, this time with a diameter of 7½ inches (18.5cm). Glue them to one end of the cylinder. Make a base from two 9 inch (22.5cm) squares of cardboard, with side pieces 2 inches (5cm) high.

For the top, cut an 11 inch (27.5cm) square of cardboard. Using compasses and leaving 1½ inches (4cm) at the middle of each side, mark and cut curves from the corners. Bend a length of cardboard along one of the curves. Mark the length of the side, then complete the shape, finishing in a 3 inch (7.5cm) circle at each end, as shown. Cut four, and assemble as shown.

To fill the gaps at the rounded ends, cut strips of cardboard 1½ inches (4cm) wide and tape them in position. To finish the top, glue two more 7 inches (17.5cm) squares to the top of the column. Cut two 11 inch (27.5cm) squares of cardboard and join them with sides 2½ inches (6cm) high. Add this to the base of the column.

Cover the column with six layers of papier mâché, not forgetting the bottom. Then apply two coats of water-based paint.

This attractive plant display column could be brought outside on a fine day, but it is really intended for indoor use. First, make a cylinder, 12 inches (30cm) high and with a diameter of 6 inches (15cm), using two circles and a rectangle of cardboard. Use white glue and tape to assemble the cylinder.

Paint to suit your décor. This particular column was painted with pink wood primer, which gave it an attractive matt finish. It was then stippled with a piece of screwed-up rag soaked in dark gray wood primer.

46

When dry, use a pencil to draw a line dividing the shape into two equal halves. You can erase any unsatisfactory attempts. When you are satisfied, cut along the pencil line with a sharp knife.

Lay each half on cardboard and mark around it, then cut out a back.

Paint the matching edges with white glue, then hold them together with brown tape. Papier mâché the back and edges of each vase, applying three layers over the back and as far inside as you can reach, all at one go. Leave them to dry, preferably on a wire cooling rack in a warm place.

With this technique, you can make two attractive wall vases at the same time. First cover a balloon with five layers of papier mâché. When this has dried, pierce the string end of the balloon and remove.

Cut a small hole at the back of each vase, about 1 inch (2.5cm) down from the top. Sand and seal the vases and give them two coats of water-based paint. The vases can then be decorated, either with black and white water-based paint, finished with three coats of acrylic varnish; or with gouache, finished with polyurethane.

Cut into that end, as shown, gently bending out the resulting teeth. Cover this toothed edge with two layers of 3 inch (7.5cm) square papier mâché. Let this dry overnight, then add another two layers.

Once the parts are roughly taped together, go over them again with brown tape, covering all the joints and edges. This gives a better finish.

Measure the length of a shelf front and the top. Make paper templates for a shelf frill and scroll top. Using a craft knife, cut three shelf frills (these are used singly) and three scrolls (joined together, like the shelves).

Again with brown tape, add the break-top scroll and shelf frills to the unit.

Laying the unit on cardboard, mark and cut out a back piece. Attach this with white glue and brown tape. For greater stability, add a base, again using three thicknesses of cardboard. Cut the base pieces ⅜ inch (1cm) wider and ¾ inch (2cm) longer than the existing base. Also, for fun, glue three table tennis balls to the top. Apply six layers of papier mâché.

This antique-style shelving unit makes a charming showcase for small ornaments. The main frame of the shelves is made from cardboard. Cut twelve pieces measuring 14 by 2¾ inches (35 by 7cm) and six pieces 16 by 2¾ inches (40 by 7cm.) The shelves and sides are all made from three layers each, fitted together as shown and held with brown tape.

When dry, give the unit two coats of water-based paint and leave it to dry. Paint with yellow ocher gouache and then add the lines in alizarin crimson. To complete the unit, give it two coats of mahogany-stained varnish. Further coats will give a progressively darker effect, if liked.

To make this clock, you will require a clock movement with a screw fitting behind the hands, available from craft suppliers. The top and base are octagons, made by trimming the corners from 8 inch (20cm) squares of cardboard; the side pieces are all 10 inches (25cm) high, cut to the width of the octagon sides. Cut crenelations into the top edge of the side pieces. Cut a circle from the base.

Tape the pieces together as shown, taping the circle that was cut from the base to the front, to become the clock face.

To make the spire, cut four isosceles triangles, with a base of 3¾ inches (9cm) and a height of 8 inches (20cm).

Tape the pieces together and tape the spire to the tower.

Apply six layers of papier mâché. When dry, give the tower two coats of water-based paint and then a coat of sand-colored gloss paint. Dry-brush a dark brown gloss over the sand to create the stony look. Make a hole in the front and fit the clock movement, adding the hands once this is secure. Paint the numerals, winding the hands round to see where they should go.

## POTATO PRINT PILLOWS

Y ou probably think of potato printing as something you used to do in kindergarten – well, think again! It can be used to great effect when decorating soft furnishings for the home. Cut a potato in half and draw the design onto one half with a felt-tip pen. Now cut around the motif so that the design stands proud of the background.

Paint some fabric paint onto the potato motif with a brush. Stamp off any excess paint onto some waste paper, then print the motif onto your chosen fabric, leaving plenty of space for a second and even a third motif.

Cut another simple motif from the other half of the potato. Apply the color as before and print onto the fabric. When the fabric has dried, iron on the back to fix the paints. Your fabric is now ready to be made up into pillows.

## "QUILT" PILLOWS

T hese pillows are based on designs taken from American patchwork quilts. With a soft pencil, copy the design onto tracing paper. Then position the trace, pencil marks down, over your chosen fabric. Transfer the image onto the fabric by tracing over the back of the design.

When the design is on the material, go over it with a pencil if the image is not strong enough. Apply the first color using a fabric felt-tip pen.

Fill in the other colors. If you are using alternate colors, as on these leaves, it is a good idea to mark each leaf with the correct color so you don't make a mistake halfway through. Iron on the back to fix the design and make the fabric up into pillows.

The inspiration for this vase comes from a beautiful piece of Victorian embroidery. The designs are similar except that the white and black have been reversed. Instead of white stalks on a black background, there are black stalks on a white background. You can either copy this design, or find a similar piece of embroidery to copy.

As it is always difficult to paint directly onto a curved surface, first draw the design onto the vase using a Chinagraph pencil.

Color in the design with ceramic paints, mixing the various colors together to get the right shades. Use very fine paint brushes for the stalks and slightly thicker ones for the leaves and flowers. Clean the brushes carefully between each color.

Decorate a plain ceramic planter with bamboo stems and leaves, painted in a Chinese style. You will need green and yellow ceramic paint and green and black glass paint. Paint wide vertical lines of green around your pot. Use a ¾ inch (20cm) decorator's brush and both the glass and the ceramic paints to give different depths of color. Make the lines uneven and slightly crooked.

Add yellow highlights to some of the green stripes. Mix together some green and a little black paint. With a fine pointed brush, paint slightly curved horizontal lines at intervals across the vertical lines. Finally, using a soft pointed Chinese art brush and the green/black mix, paint groups of leaves radiating out from the stems.

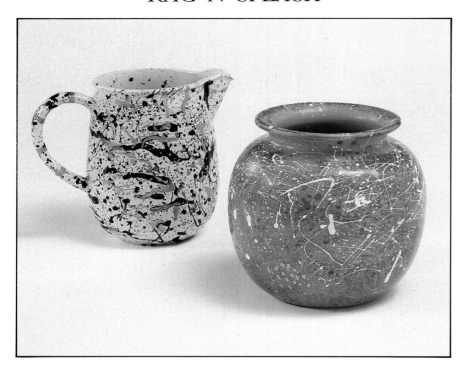

An elegant but inexpensive vase is transformed with the simple use of a sponge and some ceramic paints. Take a small piece of natural sponge and dip it into some mineral spirit. Squeeze the sponge out and lightly dip it into a saucer of ceramic paint. Dab excess paint onto a piece of waste paper, then apply the color to the vase with a light dabbing motion.

Sponge the whole of the vase, leaving space for a second color, and reapplying paint to the sponge as necessary. Use a second sponge to apply the next color, making sure to overlap the colors for an even finish. As an alternative to ceramic paints, you could use high gloss gold lacquer and regular water-based paint.

With a combination of ragging and flicking you can transform a plain china vase or pitcher into a work of art. You will need a piece of cloth for the ragging, a couple of fine artists' brushes, and some ceramic paints. Dip the rag into one of the paints and then blot it onto some waste paper to remove any excess paint. Now begin to dab paint onto the vase.

Leave gaps between the dabs of paint to let the background color show through. When you have evenly covered the surface, leave it to dry. Now spatter the vase with white ceramic paint, flicking the paint on with a fine brush. Once again, leave to dry.

Finally, apply some gold ceramic paint with a fine paint brush, forming clusters of little gold dots across the surface of the vase. Be sure to clean your brush thoroughly in turpentine when you have finished.

Using a pencil or a medium-size knitting pin, lightly score across each side piece, from one inner angle to the other. Paint first one side and then the other of all five pieces with white glue. This will seal the card and help to prevent warping.

When the pieces are dry, paint all the sides and base edges with white glue. Fit the pieces together as shown, using strips of brown tape to hold them in place. Leave the vase to dry overnight.

Layering the pieces alternately vertically and horizontally, cover the vase, inside and out, with three layers of papier mâché, each piece approximately 1 by 3 inches (2.5 by 7.5cm). When dry, sand and then seal with thinned white glue.

Paint the vase all over with white water-based paint. The first layer may crack, but when this has dried, apply a second layer, which should be flat and white.

To use for flower arranging, insert a glass inside the papier mâché vase. From cardboard, cut one piece 5 inches (12.5cm) square and four pieces 10 by 5 inches (25 by 12.5cm). On each long side of the four pieces, mark a point 2 inches (5cm) up from the bottom and 1 inch (2.5cm) in. Draw straight lines from the corners to this point and cut as shown, to make angled sides.

Use the thinned glue to apply pieces of torn colored tissue paper, inside and out, and then pieces of cut aluminum foil candy wrappers. When dry, apply three layers of acrylic varnish, putting your hand inside the vase for the outer layers, and standing it on its base for the inside. Finish by varnishing the bottom.

Standing the shape on its base, mark the top of the pitcher by holding a bowl over the top, placing it at a slight angle. To make the lip of the pitcher, first cut a triangle of paper and make a fold down the center. Hold this nose shape against the pitcher, and mark the profile of the pitcher on the paper. Trim and fit until the two sit together easily.

Use the template to cut a card lip, adding tags as shown, and cut a corresponding notch from the pitcher. Sketch a handle for the pitcher. Cut one from cardboard, making adjustments for a good fit as necessary, then cut three more identical handles from cardboard. From thin card, cut two more handles, with tabs at either end.

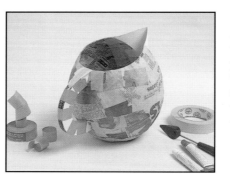

Glue and tape the handle together. Hold it next to the pitcher and mark the top and bottom, then cut slits and push the tabs through, gluing them to the inside with epoxy resin glue (use a spatula for the lower tags). Also attach the lip. Hold with masking tape until the glue has dried.

This elegant decorative pitcher is painted with a 1950s-style design. To make it, papier mâché a balloon. Then mark the bottom (a reel of brown tape was used here), and cut out the section to create a flat base.

When the glue is dry, remove the tape. Apply three layers of papier mâché, all at one go, to the handle and the lip, covering all tags. Sand and seal the pitcher, then apply two coats of white water-based paint.

Supporting the balloon shape in a bowl and using strips approximately 2 by 6 inches (5 by 15cm), cover the hole with four layers of papier mâché, applied at one go. Leave the shape to dry overnight.

Draw the pattern in pencil and then paint with gouache, starting with the palest shade and ending with black. Finish with a coat of matt polyurethane varnish.

These two candlesticks are shaped like pyramids and marbled. From cardboard, cut eight rectangles measuring 7 by 4 inches (17.5 by 10cm). On the short side of each, measure in 1 inch (2.5cm) from each corner and mark a line down to the lower corner. Cut as shown, angling all eight rectangles. Also cut four 2 inch (5cm) squares. Glue and tape the eight pieces into two pyramids.

For each pyramid, mark the shape of the bottom on cardboard and cut out. Take a 1½ inch (4cm) length of cardboard tube, such as the inner tube from a roll of freezer bags. Using scissors, cut ¼ inch (6mm) nicks at ⅛ inch (3mm) intervals around one end. Also cut a circle the diameter of the tube from one small square of card, then glue it to a complete square.

Using white glue and brown tape, fix the bases to the pyramids. Then fix the candle holder tubes into the recessed top pieces. Finally, fix the tops in position. When both candlesticks have been assembled, paint all over with a coat of thinned white glue, to prevent warping.

Cover with three layers of papier mâché, applied all at one go. When dry, sand and seal again with thinned white glue. Apply two coats of white water-based paint. Then paint with thinned black gouache, adding touches of blue and green while the black is still wet. This overall wash forms the base for the marbling.

Next, apply stronger black lines of gouache, flattening the loaded brush on the edge of the paint pot to shape the end into a chisel. Add more lines with a gold felt-tip pen. Give the candle holder three layers of gold poster paint. Finish with matt polyurethane varnish, brushing along the gold pen lines with light strokes. Give the finished candlesticks a coat of fire retardant.

Glue and tape together the matching squares. Center the smaller square on the flat side of the larger, and glue and tape it to make the lid. Coat a rubber ball with petroleum jelly and apply four layers of papier mâché, using fairly small pieces. To check for gaps, let the paper dry between layers.

Apply three layers of papier mâché to the box at one time, using pieces measuring about 1 by 3 inches (2.5 by 7.5cm). When the ball is dry, mark the circumference and cut around it.

Remove the papier mâché and immediately glue the two halves together, holding them with masking tape. When dry, cover the join with two more layers of small pieces.

Glue the dry ball to the lid recess with epoxy resin glue. Sand and seal the box and lid, then apply two coats of white water-based paint.

This marbled box has a golden handle on the lid. From cardboard, cut four (side) pieces 6 by 4 inches (15 by 10cm), two (lids) 5½ inches (13.8cm) square and two (inside lids) 3½ inches (9cm) square. Join the sides with white glue and tape, then mark and cut out a base. Join this to the sides. At the center of one of the large squares, mark and cut a hole 1 inch (2.5cm) in diameter.

Paint the inside of the box and lid with gouache. Decorate the outside with brown and orange chalk, then brush all over with clear water. Repeat two or three times for depth of color. Give the ball three coats of gold poster paint. Finish with a coat of matt polyurethane varnish.

This would make an excellent holder for pencils or brushes. Cover your chosen shape – perhaps a plastic cream or yogurt tub – with petroleum jelly. Apply five layers of papier mâché to the outside at one time. Use strips measuring about 1½ by 6 inches (4 by 15cm), setting each new layer at right angles to the last.

When the papier mâché has dried, mark down the center line on each side. Cut with a sharp knife down the sides but not across the bottom, slightly sliding the blade under the paper to help to release the paper shape.

Remove any traces of petroleum jelly with a cotton swab and mineral spirit. Immediately paint the cut edges with white glue. Hold them together with masking tape until the glue has dried. Remove the tape and apply another couple of layers of papier mâché, inside and out.

You could simply bind the edge, but this rolled edge is created with paste-soaked pieces of paper measuring about 3 inches (7.5cm) square. Work around the edge, holding two of these rolls against the outside edge of the beaker and binding them in place with 1 by 4 inch (2.5 by 10cm) strips.

When the edge has dried, sand and seal the beaker. Then apply two coats of white emulsion. First draw the pattern on the surface with a pencil, then paint with gouache colors. Paint the black lines of gouache last. Finish with a coat of matt polyurethane varnish.

# GOLDEN HONEY POT

T ransform a rather plain ceramic honey pot into something striking. Using a fine paint brush and black ceramic paint, paint some bees onto the lid of the pot. If you are worried about painting free-hand, first draw the bees on with a Chinagraph pencil. And if you are not even sure how to draw a bee, copy one from a picture.

Now paint the stripes with black ceramic paint. If, like this one, your pot is ridged, use the raised surface as a guide for your lines of paint. Otherwise, you can use strips of masking tape to mask off those areas which are to be yellow. In order not to smudge the work, you may find it easier to paint the lower half first and then leave it to dry before painting the top half.

When all the black has dried, apply the yellow ceramic paint, carefully filling in the bee's striped body with a fine brush. Fill the pot with honey and have a nice breakfast!

# TORN TAPE PLATE

C reate a stunning design by using a very simple but effective design technique, known as masking. Cut a strip of masking tape the width of your plate. Then very carefully rip it in half lengthwise, creating an uneven edge. Place the two torn pieces back to back across the center of the plate. Then add more double strips of tape on either side, leaving gaps in between each set.

When you have covered the plate in torn tape lines, make sure that all the edges are stuck down properly. Apply ceramic paint to the exposed areas, using a dabbing motion so that the paint does not seep under the tape.

Leave the plate to dry for at least 24 hours before carefully removing the tape. Clean up any smudged edges using a rag dipped in mineral spirit, then apply a coat of ceramic varnish. The black lines on a white background gives a striking "zebra stripe" effect, but other color combinations look equally attractive, so try experimenting a little.

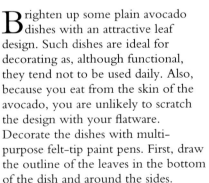

**B**righten up some plain avocado dishes with an attractive leaf design. Such dishes are ideal for decorating as, although functional, they tend not to be used daily. Also, because you eat from the skin of the avocado, you are unlikely to scratch the design with your flatware. Decorate the dishes with multi-purpose felt-tip paint pens. First, draw the outline of the leaves in the bottom of the dish and around the sides.

Fill in half the leaves with the same color to make a strong image. Then create a broken line of color around the rim of the dish as shown. For variety, paint each dish in the set a different color. When the paint is dry, apply a protective coat of ceramic varnish.

**W**ho's been eating my porridge . . . and left footprints all over my plate? You can have great fun decorating china like this, using bird prints, paw prints, Wellington boots, or even human footprints. To make the paw print plate, first draw a spiral onto the plate as shown with a Chinagraph pencil.

Using the spiral as a guide, paint the outline of the prints in black ceramic paint: you will need a very fine paint brush for this. Once the paint has dried, erase all trace of the Chinagraph line.

Color the center of the paws with a brightly colored ceramic paint. When the plate is completely dry, finish off with a protective coat of ceramic varnish.

Choose a simple motif, such as holly, mistletoe, or bells, and create your own unique festive tea service. For this attractive holly design, you will need plain white china, red and green ceramic paint, and a fine paint brush. Paint the outlines of the holly leaves with green paint, grouping the leaves together in threes. Now fill in the leaf outlines with more green paint.

Join up the leaves with garlands of red berries made by applying dots of red ceramic paint with a very fine brush. Also add clusters of berries at the base of the leaves. When the paint is completely dry, finish off with a coat of ceramic varnish. To complete the picture, you can even paint the motif onto the corner of your paper napkins.

These candlesticks are designed for those in a party mood; they are bright and fun, and especially suitable for a teenage party. You will need some self-adhesive ring reinforcements, candlesticks, and multi-purpose felt-tip paint pens in a range of bright colors. Stick the ring reinforcements all over the candlestick as shown.

Paint the centers of the circles in various colors. Once the paint is dry, peel off the reinforcements to reveal a series of colored dots. Complete the design by painting a border line around the bottom of the stem in one of the bright colors you have been using. Finally, apply a coat of ceramic varnish.

These octagonal glasses look very stylish with a band of color rotating around the glass. You will need either ceramic or glass paint. Cut four or five strips of masking tape long enough to wind from the top of the glass down to the bottom. Stick the first strip down, then add successive strips, leaving a gap between each one.

Apply the paint to the exposed areas, holding onto the masking tape while you rotate the glass. Now leave the glass to dry.

Remove the masking tape. If some of the paint has seeped under the tape, clean it off with a cloth dipped in turpentine.

You can transform the cheapest type of wine glasses into these stylish drinking vessels with no more than a little ingenuity and some glass paints. Working from either the top or the bottom of the glass, paint on a winding plant stem using a fine brush. You may have to leave the glass to dry between painting the bulb and the base so that you do not smudge the paint.

Once the stem has dried, you can then decorate it with intricate leaves and curling tendrils. Use a very fine brush to achieve a delicate finish.

Bring the countryside into your kitchen with these attractive storage jars. Cut out a piece of paper to fit round the side of the jar. Then, using the template on page 251, draw your design onto the paper. To work out your color scheme, color the design using felt-tip pens. Trace off the design onto the jar and outline the pencil with a fine black felt-tip pen.

Color the corn with the colored felt-tip pens, leaving the middle of some of the husks the natural wood color so that the corn looks more rounded and realistic. Paint the center of some of the other husks yellow to add more interest. Do not press the pens too hard as the color will bleed.

Color in the animals and butterflies and decorate around the top edge of the jar with green, as shown in the main picture, to suggest hills. Paint the lid with swallows soaring in the sunshine. When the inks are dry, finish with a coat of polyurethane varnish to protect the color.

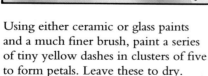

When you buy herbs in jars you are paying more for the packaging than the contents, so why not make your own storage jars and save money? Collect some old glass jars with lids and wash them in hot soapy water, removing any tough labels with a pot scourer. Dry the jars thoroughly, then use a medium-size artists' brush to paint the lids with ceramic paint.

Using either ceramic or glass paints and a much finer brush, paint a series of tiny yellow dashes in clusters of five to form petals. Leave these to dry.

Now dot the flower centers with the same color of paint you used for the lids. Add the green trellis between the flowers, using ceramic or glass paint as before. If using glass paint, you may need to apply two coats to achieve a strong color.

Crackle varnish creates an interesting "antique" finish on a prettily decorated wooden salt box. Such boxes can be purchased from specialty craft suppliers at little cost. First, draw your design in pencil onto the pieces of the box. Go over the pencil marks using a fine paint brush and black acrylic paint.

Now fill in the design using brightly colored acrylic paints, mixing and diluting them with a little water if necessary. Leave the paints to dry thoroughly before pinning the box pieces together.

Cover the box with a coat of patina varnish. Leave it to dry for between 4–12 hours and then apply a second coat. Once the second coat is dry to the touch (rather than completely dry), paint on a coat of crackle varnish. This should crackle in 15-20 minutes, leaving the box with a crazed, old appearance.

With a design "borrowed" from the turn of the century, new life has been breathed into some old kitchen scales. To transform a pair of scales, you will need gold and black ceramic paints and some gold spray paint. Clean the surface of the scales with soapy water, then sand down with fine sandpaper. Now apply a coat of black paint; you may need two coats to cover the old finish.

When the black ceramic paint has dried, paint your design in gold using a fine artists' brush. Create the outline first and then fill in with more gold paint. (You may wish to practice your design first on paper before actually applying paint to the scales.)

If the scales are purely for a decorative purpose, spray the old scoop with gold paint. If they are going to be used for food, it is probably better not to paint the scoop. Remember always to use spray paints in a well–ventilated area.

Decorate some napkin rings, and even some napkins, to match your tea or dinner service. You will need ceramic paints that match the colors of your china: in this case blue, green, and pink. First, paint the outline of the design. Use a very fine brush and be careful to make a single sweeping movement with each stroke.

When the initial coat is dry, begin to fill in the outline with a second color, carefully following the design on your plate.

Finish off with a third and, if necessary, a fourth color, letting each coat dry before applying a new one. Protect the design with a coat of ceramic varnish. If you wish to decorate your table napkins as well, follow the same procedure using fabric paints instead of ceramic ones.

Here's a design the children will love: personalized plate mats delightfully decorated with dogs, cats, or even some cute woolly sheep. Look in cards, magazines, and children's books for images to copy. Either trace your design or draw it freehand onto some paper. Cut out and draw round your motif onto a plain mat using a Chinagraph pencil.

Color in your image using multi-purpose felt-tip pens. If, after you have finished, you have left smudges on your mat, erase them with lighter fuel. Finish off with a colored border round the edge of the mat.

# GIFTS & NOVELTIES

**W**hy not have some fun restoring a battered old box and, rather than simply giving it a coat of paint, transform it with a striking black and white leopard skin design? As you can see, this box was originally in a very shabby state with its chipped paint and peeling labels.

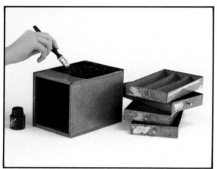

First sand the box down, then give it a coat of black ceramic paint. This paint is suitable for metals and gives a shiny finish. If your box is wooden, you can use acrylic paints instead.

When the black paint has dried, paint the leopard skin markings in white ceramic paint. Look at pictures of leopards and other animals with interesting markings for inspiration. If your box is for stationery, you can even paint some black pens to match.

**H**ere's another idea for the kids – a customized school bag and vacuum flask. All you need are the case and vacuum flask and some multi-purpose felt-tip paint pens. Choose striking color combinations such as the red, white, and black used here. In a strong sweeping movement, paint a deep wavy line using a thick pen. Change pens and finish the curve in a contrasting color.

Add more wavy lines, alternating colors as before. Then, using a fine pen, draw zigzag lines cutting across the curved lines. Finally, change pens and draw more zigzag lines in the second color.

There is no excuse for mislaying letters with this smart letter rack. From thick mounting board cut a rectangle 9½ by 3¼ inches (24 by 8cm) for the front and 9½ by 4 inches (24 by 10cm) for the back. Diagonally trim away the top corners and cover one side of each piece with giftwrap.

Cut giftwrap slightly smaller than the front and back sections and glue in position on the wrong side. Take a piece of wood 9½ inches (24cm) long by 1¼ inches (3cm) wide and ⅛ inches (1cm) thick. Cover the wood with colored paper.

Cut a rectangle of mounting board 10½ by 2¾ inches (27 by 7cm) for the base and cover with colored paper. Use a strong glue to stick the front to one narrow edge of the wood keeping the lower edges level. Glue the back to the other side in the same way. Finish the letter rack by gluing this upper section centrally to the base.

This pretty little frame is perfect for standing on a dressing table. Firstly, sand the frame until it is smooth and then give it a coat of white acrylic paint. Apply a second coat of paint if necessary and, when dry, draw the design with a soft pencil. Paint the design using acrylic paint in soft blues and grays with the flower centers in bright yellow.

Remove the backing and the glass and give the frame a protective coat of polyurethane varnish.

Transform a pear-shaped cutting board into a novelty blackboard for the children. All you need is blackboard paint and some acrylic paint for the leaves. First draw the leaf design in pencil onto the board.

Now paint the board with the blackboard paint, using a fine brush to paint round the leaf design. The board may need more than one coat of blackboard paint, so let the first coat dry before applying the second.

When the paint is dry, apply the color to the leaves with a fine brush. Finally, give the leaves a coat of varnish to make them shine. Do not varnish the black paint!

Create a unique gift for the man in your life by decorating a pair of boxer shorts with fabric felt-tip pens. Draw your design onto paper first, referring to the template on page 245 if you wish to create this busy design. Work out your color scheme by coloring in your design with felt-tip pens.

Place a piece of card between the front and the back of the shorts to stretch the waist band and stop the paint seeping through. Draw the design onto the fabric using a fine fabric felt-tip pen. If you don't feel confident drawing the design straight on in pen, trace it on in pencil first.

Color in the design in bright colors, using either fabric felt-tip pens or fabric paint and a brush. To fix the paint, iron on the back of the fabric once your design is complete.

This colorful design is applied using transfer paints. As well as the paints, you will also need a piece of nonabsorbent paper, such as tracing paper, and an iron. Draw your design onto the paper, referring to the template on page 245, and making sure that it will fit onto the scarf you wish to decorate.

Color in your design with the transfer paints in the same way as you would using any water-based paints. Mix the colors together and dilute them with water as you wish.

Leave the paints to dry for an hour, then place the design face down on the scarf so that the paint is against the fabric. Set your iron to the cotton setting and iron on the back of the paper for one minute so that the color is transferred. When the paper has cooled, remove it from the scarf.

These Grecian-style T-shirts are decorated with a paint that expands upon heating, so that the design is raised above the surface of the fabric. First, draw your design onto a piece of paper. Then stick the design onto a piece of cardboard and stretch the T-shirt over the card, fastening the fabric down with masking tape. Trace the design onto the T-shirt using the "expanding medium" paint.

Leave the paint to dry for 20 to 30 minutes before fixing it. This can be done by ironing the reverse of the design for 15 seconds (using a silk or wool setting). The other way to set and expand the paint is to use a hair drier.

Relive the memories of peaceful vacations by the sea with this seascape collage. Tear strips of tissue paper – pale blue and white for the sky and pale green and turquoise for the sea. Cut out a circle of orange paper for the sun. Arrange the strips horizontally across a piece of white cardboard to get an idea of the finished picture.

Stick the top two strips across the cardboard with spray glue. Leave a gap, then apply the fourth strip. Glue the sun on top and then the third strip across the sun. Continue down the card. Cut straight across the strips that will meet at the horizon. Tear slithers of white frosted paper and glue across the bottom of the picture as surf.

Cut a jagged cliff shape from brown crepe paper and glue to the collage. Glue a slither of green tissue paper on top for grass. Trim away the excess paper around the edges of the card. Cut out three seagulls from black paper and glue onto the sky.

Give your home a period touch with this classic decoration. You can use a clear profile sketch or a photograph as a basis for your picture. Make a tracing of the outline and place it face down on the back of a piece of black paper. Redraw the design to transfer it.

Cut out the motif with a pair of small, sharp scissors and glue the design onto white paper. Trim the paper to fit your frame. Place the picture in the frame and glue a small ribbon bow to the top.

Stylish and original stationery is expensive to buy, but this delicate design is cheap and easy to produce. Draw a simple motif on tracing paper, then retrace the design on the other side. Place your drawing on the top left-hand corner of a sheet of writing paper about ⅜ inch (1cm) inside the edges. Redraw the motif to transfer it to the writing paper.

Glass paperweights such as these are available in kit form from craft stores. To work out a mosaic picture, draw a grid of squares about ³⁄₁₆ inch (4mm) apart. Trace around the paperweight template onto the grid and draw a design. Color the picture as a guide for the finished mosaic.

Now prick along the lines with a needle or pin. You may find it helpful to practice on a scrap of paper first to judge how far apart the pinpricks should be.

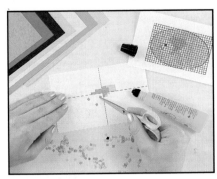

Cut out tiny squares of colored paper the same size as the grid squares. Draw a cross on a piece of paper to help keep the mosaic squares straight. Spread paper glue thinly along part of one line and press the squares in place. Nudge them into position with scissors or tweezers. Follow the grid design and glue on all the squares.

Erase the pencil lines, then trim away the corner of the paper to echo the shape of the design. Pinprick a coordinating motif on the matching envelope flap.

Use the paperweight template to cut the mosaic to fit the paperweight. Turn the paperweight upside down and lay the mosaic in the hollow. Peel the paper off the self-adhesive felt backing and carefully stick it over the back of the paperweight enclosing the mosaic.

The right mount can really enhance a picture. Buy a plain cardboard mount to fit your picture. Draw a ⅜ inch (1cm) wide border around the window with a pencil. Cut four ⅜ inch (1cm) wide strips of marbled paper. Spray the back of one strip with spray glue and place on the border. Cut off the ends diagonally at the corners with a craft knife.

Apply the other strips to the mount, cutting the ends to meet diagonally in a mitered corner.

To make these smart frames, cut two pieces of mounting board 10 by 7½ inches (25cm by 19cm). Cut a window 7 by 4½ inches (17cm by 11cm) in the center of one piece. Cut two pieces of giftwrap to cover the frames. Lay the window mount on the wrong side of one piece and cut a window in the giftwrap, leaving a ¾ inch (2cm) margin. Snip to the corners and glue the margins down.

To complete the mount, draw a line each side of the border with a fine-tipped gold pen.

Cover the back of the frame with giftwrap. Cut two ⅜ inch (1cm) wide strips of mounting board 7¼ inches (18cm) long and one strip 8½ inches (22cm) long. Cover with paper and glue to the wrong side of the back just inside three of the edges. Spread glue on the strips and carefully place the front of the frame on top, checking that the outer edges are level.

Cut a rectangle of mounting board 7¼ by 2¼ inches (18cm by 6cm) for the stand. Score across the stand 2 inches (5cm) from one end. Cover the stand with giftwrap and glue the second end to the back. Ensure that the other end is level with either the long or short side, depending on whether your photograph is in landscape or portrait form. Bend the stand outward.

Papier-mâché is very durable and can be made in many ways. This traditional method uses a paste of flour and water. Tear up wallpaper liner paper into small pieces. Then grease the inside of a small bowl with petroleum jelly. Brush the paper pieces with paste and stick them inside the bowl, starting at the center and working outward.

Revive the Victorian hobby of découpage and decorate a box with pretty paper pictures. Cut out suitable pictures from greeting cards or magazines, or use reproductions of Victorian prints.

Build up three layers of papier-mâché and leave to dry overnight. Apply at least four more layers. When the papier-mâché is completely dry, remove it from the bowl mold. Trim the top edge level with a pair of scissors. Paint the bowl with a craft paint, sanding between coats. Cut colored tissue paper into small triangles.

Arrange the pictures on the box and then stick them in place with spray glue. Smooth in place.

Stick the triangles to the bowl with a clear varnish such as PVA medium. Once the bowl is decorated, coat it inside and out with the varnish. Line the bowl with tissue paper and fill it with pretty bathroom accessories.

Apply a thin coat of clear gloss varnish all over the box and lid. Leave to dry and then sand lightly with fine sandpaper. Build up about six layers of varnish, sanding the box between each coat.

These amusing finger puppets are sure to entertain your friends. Use the template on page 244 to cut out the dancer in pale pink cardboard. Cut out the dress in shiny, deep pink cardboard and glue to the puppet. Next cut an 3 inch (8cm) diameter circle from the center of a white paper doily for a petticoat and glue to the dress with spray glue.

Color the hair, draw the eyes, and lightly mark the nose with a black felt-tip pen. Draw the mouth with a red felt-tip pen and rouge the cheeks with a red colored pencil.

Mark the finger hole positions on the petticoat and carefully cut through all the layers with a craft knife.

Quick and simple to make, this place mat will brighten up the dinner table. Cut a wavy-edged rectangle of blue cardboard 14 by 10 inches (35 by 25cm). Cut a row of wavy slits lengthwise across the mat with a craft knife.

Cut wavy-edged strips 9 inches (23cm) long from green cardboard. Weave the first strip in and out of the slits close to one end. Weave in the remaining strips, starting each alternate strip at the next slit up.

On the back, lift up the ends of the strips and glue to the mat. Make a matching coaster from a small wavy-edged square of cardboard.

Using white glue and brown tape, sandwich the two front pieces and then the two back pieces together. Attach the support to the back of the frame, checking that the angle will be correct when the frame is standing, and that it will not lean too far back. Seal with thinned white glue to avoid warping.

Attach string to the front of the frame with epoxy resin glue. The three bobbles at the bottom edge are made from crumpled balls of masking tape.

Give the front and back three layers of papier mâché each, pushing the paper carefully around the string. To avoid warping, peg the front and back together when they are almost dry.

This attractive frame is designed to hold a standard 4 by 6 inch (10 by 15cm) print. From cardboard, cut pieces as shown in the diagram.

When both pieces are fully dry, sand the back and also the back of the frame's front. Then give them two coats of water-based paint. Joining the back and front together, apply two layers of papier mâché down the sides and along the lower edge.

Sand and seal, then paint the finished frame with water-based paint. Gold poster paint is used for the gilding. The remainder of the frame is painted with gouache and then sealed with clear varnish designed for gouaches and watercolors.

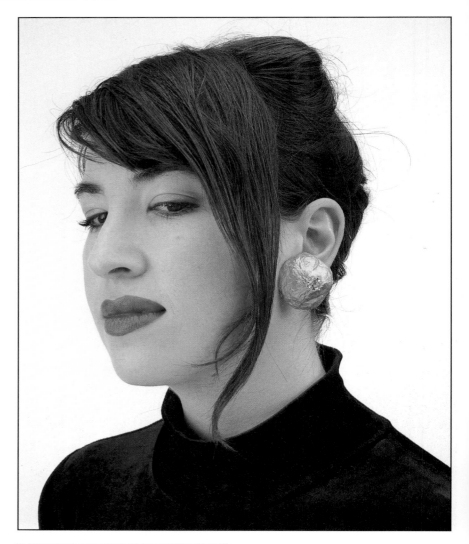

The fixings for these can be bought at bead stores. The balls for the earrings are made from broadsheet newspaper, crumpled up and left in paste to soak overnight. The three sizes are made from a half, a quarter, and an eighth of a page respectively. When soaked, squeeze out excess paste and shape them into firm balls. Leave to dry.

Make indents for the glass jewels with a countersink. Paint the dangly earrings with black water-based paint and the gold ones with poster paint, finishing the latter with polyurethane varnish. Use a wooden pick to put a drop of white glue in each indent, and push in a glass jewel. Connect up the dangling earrings and fit the ear wires. Attach clips to the other pair with epoxy resin glue.

Use a hat pin or similar sharp point to make holes for the connecting hooks of the dangling earrings: one hook for the largest ball, and one at both the top and bottom of the middle and small sizes. Use epoxy resin glue to secure the hooks. For the clip-on earrings, make one large ball, then cut it in half when dry.

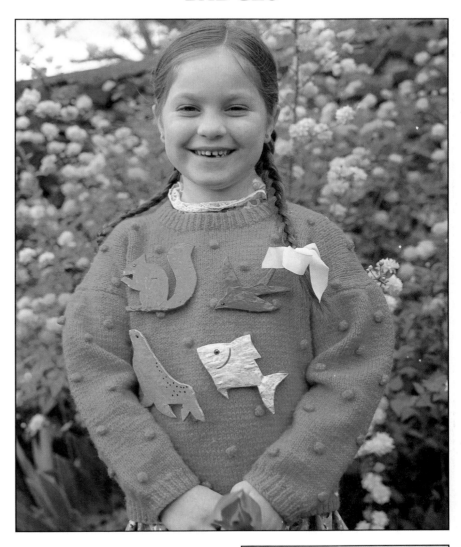

On thin cardboard, draw a circle with a radius of 2 inches (5cm) and cut out a quarter circle. Bend this into a cone shape and tape over the join. Apply from two to three layers of papier mâché. When this has dried, attach an ornamental pin along the length of the shape, using epoxy resin glue. Make sure that the pointed end of the pin lies at the pointed end of the shape.

Apply two coats of water-based paint, then paint with yellow gouache. Add blue spots, then attach a yellow bead to the pointed end of the cone, using epoxy resin glue. Varnish inside and out with two coats of semi-matt polyurethane varnish. To prolong the life of your flower and hold it in place, pack a dampened tissue around the stem inside the cone.

There are many sources you can use for animal badges, ranging from nature books to cookie cutters. When you have chosen your shapes, draw the outlines on cardboard. Using a craft knife, cut out the shapes. Apply four layers of papier mâché to each side.

Using epoxy resin glue, attach a brooch pin to the back of each shape. Apply two coats of water-based paint, then paint the shapes with gouache colors. Add simple black eyes with white highlights. Finish with two coats of polyurethane varnish.

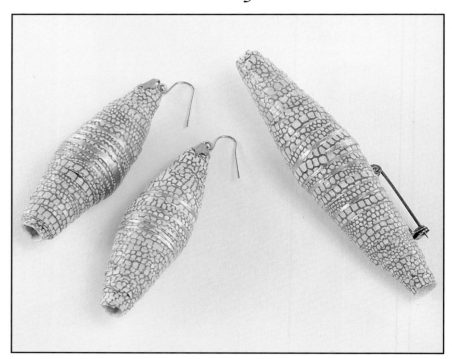

This bangle and matching necklace are made from papier mâché. You will need suitable molds for each – a small dishwashing liquid bottle is the right size for the bangle and a garden stick is ideal for the beads. Cover the stick and 2 inches (5cm) at the end of the bottle with petroleum jelly. This stops the papier mâché sticking to the mold.

Tear paper into small strips. Wallpaper liner paper was used for the bangle and newspaper for the necklace. Mix polyvinyl acetate (PVA) medium (available at artists' suppliers) with a little water to thin it. Dip a brush in the solution, then pick up a strip with the brush and press it onto the mold. Cover the petroleum jelly, overlapping the strips. Apply four layers and leave to dry.

Build up the layers to about ¼ inch (5mm) thick. Leave to dry overnight. Remove the jewelry, trim the bangle to 1¼ inches (3cm) wide with a craft knife and cut beads 1¼ inches (3cm) long. Tear giftwrap into small strips and apply to jewelry with the thinned PVA solution. Apply two coats of PVA medium as varnish. Thread the beads onto cord.

Believe it or not, this jewelry is made of paper. For each earring cut a long triangle of snakeskin-effect paper (available from specialist artists' suppliers) 30 inches (76cm) long with a 2¼ inch (6cm) wide base. Also cut a triangle from gold giftwrap 29 inches (75cm) long with a 2 inches (5cm) wide base. Using PVA medium, stick the giftwrap centrally to the wide end of the snakeskin piece.

Spread petroleum jelly on a length of wood dowel to stop the paper sticking to the wood. Starting at the wide end, roll the triangles tightly around the dowel, brushing with PVA medium as you go. Give the beads a final coat of the medium as a varnish. Leave to dry, then gently remove the dowel.

Pierce a hole through the top of each earring and attach a triangle wire. Fix a small jump ring to the triangle wire with a pair of pliers. Attach an earring hook to the ring. The brooch is made in the same way with wider triangles of snakeskin and gold paper. Glue a pin to the back of the brooch. Craft shops sell jewelry components.

Drop two or three colors onto the water and swirl together with the end of a paint brush. Cut plain paper to fit the tray. Wearing rubber gloves, start at one end of the tray and lower the paper onto the surface of the water so it can pick up the pattern. Carefully lift up the paper.

Leave the paper to dry overnight on newspaper. You can remove the paint from the tray by drawing strips of newspaper across the surface of the water.

The marbled paper can be used in many ways. Here, a plain book takes on a sophisticated look when given a jacket. Cut a rectangle of marbled paper large enough to wrap around the book with a 1 inch (2.5cm) margin on all sides. Wrap the paper around the book; then open the cover and glue the paper inside the opening edges.

Prop the book up so the jacket is open at a right angle. Snip the paper each side of the spine and stick the top and bottom margin inside the jacket, folding under the corners.

There are many methods for marbling paper but this way needs little equipment. Fill a shallow tray with water. Put spots of enamel paint on the water with a paint brush. If they sink, the paint is too thick and needs thinning with some mineral spirit. If they disperse into a faint film, it is too thin and should be mixed with more paint.

Push the paper at the ends of the spine between the spine and the pages with the points of a pair of scissors. Arrange jewelry stones on the cover and use a strong glue to stick them in place. Cut two pieces of paper to fit inside the covers and glue inside.

Blow up a long balloon, squeezing it so that you have a head-size lump at one end. Apply six layers of papier mâché, as shown, and leave to dry. Cut two triangles from cardboard, curving the sides slightly to make ears. Tape these to the head end of the balloon and papier mâché over them. Burst and remove the balloon.

Each foot is made from a piece of papier mâché balloon offcut, perhaps left over from a previous project. Cut each foot to the shape of a lemon segment and tape it to the base, bending it to fit. Papier mâché over the joins.

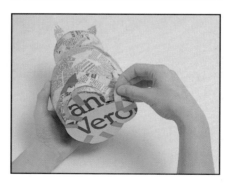

Place the cat on cardboard and draw around the base, including the feet. Cut this out and glue and tape it to the cat. Papier mâché over the join.

The tail is made from a piece of newspaper, rolled and crunched up, then curled around the body. Tape in place and then papier mâché over the tail. When dry, apply two coats of water-based paint.

Using gouache, paint the cat black, except for the tip of the tail, the inside ears, the paws, and the stomach. Draw the details carefully in pencil, then paint them – eyes yellow with black pupils and white highlights, nose flesh pink, and cheeks white with tiny black dots in rows. Finish with two coats of semi-matt polyurethane varnish.

Mark and cut an oval on one side of the large balloon, as shown.

The larger round sits in the middle of the tangle of legs, to make the body. Tape it in position, and then papier mâché over the join.

Take the small balloon and cut it in half to make the two eyes. Tape them in position and again papier mâché over the joins.

**B**low up a large balloon and apply up to eight layers of papier mâché. Also cover a small balloon. To make each leg, take a large sheet of newspaper and screw it into a long sausage. Now bend it into a loop and tape it to hold the shape. Make each leg slightly different from the others.

Apply two coats of water-based paint, and then go wild with the colors. This octopus was stippled with green and orange household gloss paint, thinned with mineral spirit. The maroon suckers were painted with modelers' enamel. The eyes were carefully painted yellow and black, with a green rim.

Tape the eight legs together. You may use a lot of tape to achieve this, but it will all add to the strength of the finished octopus. Papier mâché over the legs, using long strips of newspaper, dipped in paste and then wound around the legs. You may need to support each leg a little, to prevent the loops from sagging.

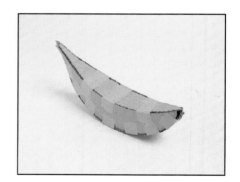

Bend the sides to fit, and tape them together. Apply four layers of papier mâché and, when dry, two coats of emulsion.

Paint the banana with yellow gouache, blending in a tiny amount of green toward the ends. Paint the stalk and the tip brown. For realism, you might add very thin brown lines partway along the edges, and small spots on each side. Finish in the same way as the orange.

For the pineapple, apply eight layers of papier mâché to a balloon. Cut a long strip of card, about 4 inches (10cm) wide, and make tapering cuts along it. Curl each leaf shape individually, then tape the strip to the pointed end of the balloon. Start at the center and work around until you have from four to five circles of leaves. If you need a second strip, make the leaves shorter.

The oranges are the simplest of these colorful ornamental fruits – all you have to do is to papier mâché a small balloon in the normal way. Burst and remove the balloon, covering the end with more papier mâché. When dry, give the shape two coats of water-based paint, then paint it with orange gouache. Finish with semi-matt polyurethane varnish.

Papier mâché over the join, but not the individual leaves. Apply two coats of water-based paint. Then paint the leaves with green gouache, made by mixing yellow and blue, so that you can vary the tones from leaf to leaf. Paint the body with honey-colored, water-based paint.

To make a banana, cut out four pieces of card, as shown. Two have curved sides and all are tapered at the top and bottom, and are longer at the stalk end. If in doubt, use a banana skin to make templates.

You may find it best to draw the segment lines in pencil before painting them, using a fine brush and light brown gouache. Build up the rest of the pattern with orange, sand, and brown. It helps if you have a real pineapple to study as you work. The painting is repetitious but well worth the effort. Finish in the same way as the orange.

Apply eight layers of papier mâché, making sure that you push the pieces into the corners to maintain the shape. Use the blunt edge of kitchen scissors or something similar to help you to ease the pieces into position.

When the ark has dried, use a craft knife to cut it away from the cardboard. Cut around the boat, from one end to the other; use a craft knife for the papier mâché, then use a table knife to cut the modeling plastic. Remove the plastic, and glue and tape the two pieces together. Papier mâché over the join.

Place the boat on a fresh piece of card, and draw around the base. Cut this shape out and glue and tape it in position. Papier mâché over the join. Apply two coats of water-based paint, then draw a large slot in the roof. Bear in mind that the slot must be large enough for the money to be shaken out as well as put in. Cut the slot with care, using a craft knife.

You will require three fairly large pieces of modeling plastic for this, so that you can make a boat shape, a rectangular block for the boat house, and a roof.

Paint the boat with gouache colors, using brown for the hull, yellow for the deck house, red for the roof, and pink for the deck. Give the deck house blue windows and a door, and add blue waves with little white crests around the hull.

Assemble the three pieces firmly together and place them on a piece of cardboard.

Add details: the dinosaur's spine ridge is made from cardboard, as are the driver's windshield and scarf. His head is a large pasted-paper ball (see page 76), and the dinosaur's eyes are smaller balls. Cut a sliver from each ball and glue this flat side in place. Papier mâché over the added shapes.

Sand and seal the shapes, and then apply two coats of white water-based paint. Also give the wheels, which can be bought from craft stores, two coats of water-based paint. When this has dried, draw the outlines of any painted pattern or details in pencil.

All the colors used here are gouache. Start with the palest, and work up to the darkest colors. It may be simplest to paint in sections, completing the top and then the underside.

Apply eight layers of papier mâché to a sausage balloon, leaving it to dry between layers. Then remove the balloon and paper over the hole. Cut two axles – long enough to hold the wheels clear of the body – from dowel. Drill screw holes for the wheels. At one end of the body, mark an outline to carry one axle. Cut, starting small and gradually enlarging the shape. Repeat at the other end.

Finish with a coat of clear watercolor varnish, including the wheels. When dry, fix the wheels in position, using a metal washer on both sides. Take care not to make these so tight that the wheels are unable to turn.

Paint the edges of the holes and the axles with white glue. Insert the axles and hold them in place with masking tape. When the glue has set, remove the masking tape and cover the axles, where they touch the body, with at least four layers of papier mâché, using strips measuring about 1½ by 3 inches (4 by 7.5cm).

Papier mâché is a traditional material for a puppet head. First, mold pieces of modeling plastic to make the components for the head. You will need the following for the famous English puppet, Mr. Punch: a large ball for the basic head shape, a large nose, two sausage shapes for eyebrows, another larger one for the mouth, a chin, a hat, and a ruff. You will also need a jam jar to sit him on.

Once you have prepared all the component parts, assemble them together, sitting the head on the jam jar. Do not worry about slight imperfections and joins – these will be concealed beneath the papier mâché.

Using thin strips of paper, carefully papier mâché over the entire head. Make sure that it is well covered, giving it from six to ten layers. Leave it until it has dried out completely. Remove the head from the jar and carefully cut the front from the back, as shown. Cut through the papier mâché with a craft knife, and then through the modeling plastic with a table knife.

Tease the plastic out from the two halves, taking special care with the ruff and the nose. Tape the two halves back together again and papier mâché over the join. Give the finished head two coats of water-based paint, then paint the face, hat, and features with gouache. To make the flesh tint for the face, add a little red and a touch of yellow to white. Finish with a coat of varnish.

On cardboard, draw a grid of 1 inch (2.5cm) squares. Copying square for square from the diagram, draw and cut out one beak side, one feather shape, and one beak base. Using the beak side as a template, mark and cut a second beak side to make a mirror image pair.

Paint white glue along the edges of the beak pieces and secure them with brown tape. Leave the beak to dry, then attach it to the face in the same way.

Using the feather already cut, mark and cut three more feathers from cardboard to make two mirror image pairs, as shown.

Using epoxy resin glue, attach the feather pieces to the mask. Then apply from two to three layers of papier mâché to the entire mask and leave to dry. When dry, paint the mask with two successive coats of white water-based paint.

Carnival time! Here is a dramatic mask that can be adapted to fit any number of occasions. Blow up a large balloon and cover with four to six layers of papier mâché, approximately 1 by 3 inches (2.5 by 7.5cm). When these have dried, draw a mask shape, with eyes and a nose. Use a craft knife to cut out the shape and the holes.

When the white paint is dry, coat the mask with red gloss house paint. Let this dry before adding either lines of yellow gloss or a decoration of your choice. To complete the mask, make a hole at either side and thread these with black elastic, securing this with knots at the back.

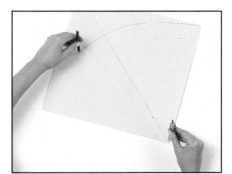

Cut out a 15 inch (38cm) square of craft paper and mark a diagonal line between two corners. Then, using a pencil and compass (or a pencil, string, and thumbtack), draw an arc between the other two corners as shown. Cut along the arc. Fold the piece along the diagonal and use it to mark out two pieces of sticky-backed plastic. Add a ½ inch (1.5cm) border to one straight edge of black plastic.

Cut out the pieces. Peel off the backing and stick the white plastic into position on the paper. Do the same with the black, leaving the backing only on the border. Form a cone, remove the border backing, and stick the edges of the cone together. Make two holes along the front join and insert red pompons (see page 19). Secure ends on inside with tape.

Feel free to act the clown in this colorful hat. First of all, make a papier mâché mold using a small mixing bowl or plastic microwave dish. When it is fully dry, remove the mold and paint it with white water-based paint. Sand down any rough edges and give it a second coat of paint.

Make the "hair" from red crêpe paper – you will need about six layers of paper, stapled together along the top. Cut the paper into even strips, stopping about 1 inch (2.5cm) from the stapled edge.

Cut out a brim from light cardboard, allowing about 2 inches (5cm) for the brim itself and an extra 1 inch (2.5cm) on the inside for attaching the brim to the crown. Make triangular cuts around the inside of the brim. Fold the triangles up and glue them to the inside of the hat. Decorate with a crêpe paper band and large colored spots. Finally, glue the hair to the inside of the hat.

This glittery version of the medieval lady's hat, with its net veil, is sure to attract a knight errant. Cut out a 15 inches (38cm) square of black craft paper. Using a white pencil and compass (or pencil, string and thumbtack), draw an arc from one corner to another. Cut along the arc.

The mold for this hat is a plastic flower pot. The one shown is for a child; an adult would need a much bigger one. Cover the flower pot in papier mâché. When it is dry, ease it off the pot and give it a coat of white water-based paint, inside and out. When this is dry, sand down any rough edges on the outside and give it another coat.

Peel the back off some sticky-backed plastic and stick the black paper down onto it. Cut out the shape, leaving a ½ inch (1.5cm) border on one straight edge. Use this to stick the hat together.

Next give the hat two coats of red paint, leaving it to dry after each coat. Make a little hole in the center of the top of the hat.

Sew tinsel around the edge of a square of net. Then attach this, with a little sticky tape, to the top of the hat. Make sure that the seam in the plastic is at the back. Finally, decorate the hat with a few stick-on silver stars.

Now make a tassel of black yarn (see the instructions on page 19). Thread it through the top of the hat, fastening it on the inside with a little sticky tape.

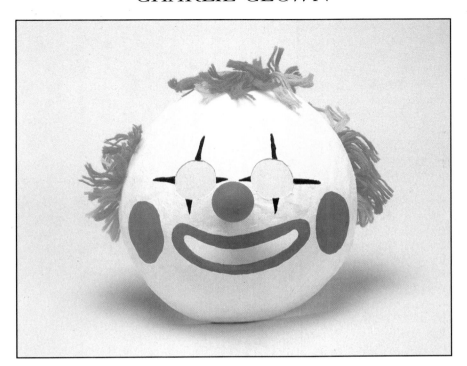

Although a bit more complicated to make than a cardboard mask, this mask will last much longer. The face is made from papier mâché; the mold is a balloon. Blow the balloon up as big as you can without bursting it, and build up the papier mâché over at least one half. When it is dry, gently let the air out of the balloon by piercing the knotted end.

Trim the mask down, cutting the pointed end into a forehead. Cut out circular eyes and a curved mouth. Now give the mold a coat of white water-based paint. Then sand it down and give it another two coats to make it as smooth a surface as possible.

For this you need a large piece of black art paper, 15 by 15½ inches (38 by 39.5cm). Mark a ½ inch (1.5cm) border at one end of the longer side so that you have a 15 inches (38cm) square. Use a compass and a white pencil to mark an arc between two corners (see page 87 for details). Cut along the arc, then spread glue on the border, and use this to join the edges of the cone together.

Use the cone to mark a circle on some black cardboard. Draw another line around the first, about 2 inches (5cm) from it, then another just 1 inch (2.5cm) inside the first line. Cut along the inner and outer lines, then make triangular cuts on the inside of the brim. Fold them up and glue them to the inside of the cone. Decorate with gold stars and moons cut from sticky-backed plastic.

Around each eye paint four slightly triangular stripes. Also paint large red lips and cheeks on either side. For the nose, paint a table tennis ball red and glue it in place. For the hair, cut short lengths of yarn and attach them to strips of sticky tape; stick these to the back of the mask. Finally, take a piece of elastic and staple it to either side. Paint over the staples with a touch more water-based paint.

For a stunning party mask, buy a ready-molded mask from a stationery or toy store. The half-mask shown here is colored with oil stencil pencils. Start with the pink; apply a little to a piece of wax paper, then pick it up on the stencil brush. Using a circular motion, cover about half the mask. Repeat with the blue, filling in the gaps and giving the eyes a semblance of eyeliner.

Next, take a short length of lace and glue it to the back of the top half of the mask, down to where the elastic is attached. Glue some strands of curling giftwrap ribbon on either side. (Curl the ribbon by running the blunt edge of a pair of scissors along it.) Lastly, glue some large sequins over the tops of the ribbons to hide the ends, and glue another one in the center of the forehead.

For the black mask, first sew some silver tinsel wire around the edge and around the eyes. Sew on some pearl beads on either side, then sew two or three gray or white feathers under the edges for an owlish look.

The basic shape can, of course, be adapted in a wide variety of ways. Draw a mask shape on cardboard. If you want both sides to be exactly the same, draw one side only on stiff paper. Cut this out, then draw around the eye and the outside, flipping it over to complete the mirror image. Cut the shape out, then gently curve it to fit the shape of the face.

To make the big nose, blow up a small balloon and cover it with four layers of papier mâché. When this has dried, slice off the end with a craft knife and remove a curved notch from one side to make room for your nose. Tape the nose to the mask, with the notch at the bottom. Make a small hole on either side of the eyes to take the elastic at a later stage.

Give the entire mask three layers of papier mâché. Follow this with two coats of white water-based paint. Using gouache colors, paint the nose red and the mask black, adding a fine red line around the edge. Finish with two coats of semi-matt polyurethane varnish. To complete the mask, thread black elastic through the holes. Adjust to fit, and then make knots behind the holes.

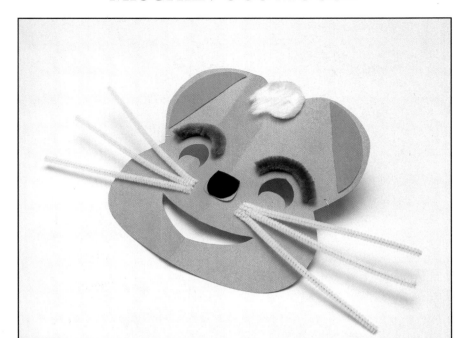

With this on, you are sure not to be recognized! First make the glasses shape from garden wire, then wind narrow ribbon all the way around them. Glue the ends in place to make sure it doesn't come undone.

This mask is simple enough for small children to put together; the only tricky bit is drawing the pattern. First take an 8 inch (20cm) square of stiff paper. Fold it in half, and open it out; then fold it in half the other way. Now draw the shape of the face on one side as shown, including the mouth and nose.

The nose is made from paper with a spongy finish. Cut a piece 3¾ by 4 inches (9 by 10cm). On the back, along one of the shorter sides, mark two lines, 1¼ inches (3cm) long and 1¼ inches (3cm) apart. Cut along these lines, so that you have three equal sections. Fold the two sides in and glue them on top of each other. Now glue the middle section over the others. Glue the edge of the nose to the glasses.

Cut around the outline, the mouth, and the nose – notice that the nose isn't cut out completely. Turn back the folded edge a little way as shown; mark in an eye and cut it out. Open out the mask.

Finally, make the beard from a piece of white fake fur, cutting a hole for the mouth. Attach a narrow strip of paper to the inside of the nose and staple either end to the back of the beard. Finish off by sticking a silver star to the glasses, just over the nose.

Cut out some pink felt ears and a black felt nose. Cut some white pipe cleaner whiskers and brown pipe cleaner eyebrows. Glue them all in place. Finally attach a piece of shirr to either side, knotting it at the back.

Here's a jaunty majorette's cap that is ideal for a fancy dress party. Cut a strip of colored cardboard 24 by 5 inches (60cm by 13cm). Cut out a peak in silver cardboard. On the wrong side, score the peak along the broken lines and make snips in the cardboard to the scored line. Bend the snipped edge upward.

Stick a 7 inch (18cm) long strip of double-sided tape in the middle of one long edge of the hat on the wrong side. Overlap the ends of the strip and lightly hold together with masking tape. Press the snipped edge of the peak onto the sticky tape. Remove the masking tape.

These conical hats are so easy to make that you will want to make one for each of your party guests. Cut a 12 inches (30cm) diameter circle of shiny cardboard for each hat and cut to the center. Cut a slice out of the circle so that the hat is not too bulky. Overlap the cut edges and glue together.

Wrap the hat around your head, overlapping the ends, then stick them together with double-sided tape. Pleat a rectangle of foil giftwrap and bind the lower edge closed with clear sticky tape, forming a fan. Glue to the front of the hat. Finally, cut out a diamond shape from silver cardboard and glue it over the fan.

There are many ways to decorate the hats – stick on gold stars or use glitter pens to draw a pattern. Another idea is to spread glue in moon shapes on the hat and then sprinkle on glitter, shaking off the excess.

Make a hole with the points of a pair of scissors on each side of the hat. Thread with hat elastic. Adjust the elastic to fit under the chin and make a knot behind the holes.

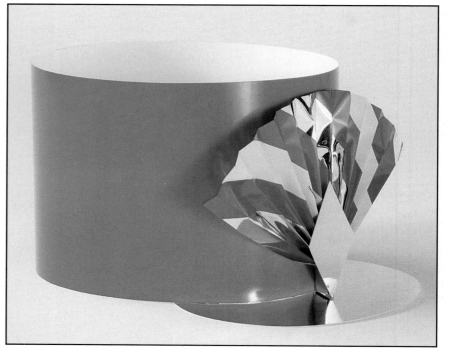

# KING OF THE JUNGLE

# FEATHERED HEADDRESS

To make this colorful headdress cut a 1½ inch (4cm) wide strip of red cardboard 24 inches (60cm) long. Cut out simple shapes from colored papers and glue to the strip.

Overlap the ends of the strip and glue together. Stick three colored quill feathers upright behind the strip with sticky tape.

This lion mask is made from papier mâché molded over a balloon. Blow up the balloon and tie a knot in the end. Tear newspaper into small pieces and then dilute polyvinyl acetate (PVA) medium with water to thin it slightly. Spread a little of the solution on the front of the balloon and cover with the newspaper pieces.

Cover one half of the balloon with about seven layers of papier mâché and leave to dry overnight. Gently pull the balloon away from the mask and trim the edges of the mask with a pair of scissors. Cut out two round holes for the eyes. Paint the mask with nontoxic, ocher-colored paint. Then paint a black nose and muzzle, as shown.

Cut six 1 inch (2.5cm) wide strips of black crêpe paper 16 inches (40cm) long. Spread paper glue along one edge and fold the strips in half. Staple three lengths together at one end and make a braid. Bind the end with embroidery thread and make another braid in the same way. Stick the braids to each side of the headdress with sticky tape.

To make the mane, cut a length of brown crêpe paper 55 by 6¼ inches (140cm by 16cm). Fold lengthwise in half. Cut a fringe along the long edges. With a needle and long length of thread, gather up the mane close to the fold. Glue the mane around the lion's face. Finally, staple a length of thin elastic to each side of the back of the mask, to fit.

This appealing children's mask is covered in soft fake fur. Using the template on page 246, cut out the cat shape in thin cardboard, fake fur, and white sticky-backed plastic. In all three, cut out the eyes.

These party bow ties lend a dashing look to a costume. For the flat tie, cut a bow-tie shape in thin cardboard, using the template on page 246. Simply cover the shape with aluminum foil, sticky-backed plastic, or felt, and attach shirr to the back.

Glue the fur piece to the cardboard one. When the glue has dried, trim the edges. Then cut out a nose in black felt and two ears in pink felt. To make the whiskers, put some glue onto a piece of cardboard and pull black thread through it as shown. When the thread dries it will be stiff.

Or make a soft fabric tie by cutting a strip of felt or other material 7 inches (18cm) square. Fold it in half, right sides together, and sew the long edges together to make a tube. Turn it right side out, and finish the raw edges by turning them in and slipstitching them.

Glue the ears in place, then cut the thread into lengths of about 4 inches (10cm). Lay them where the nose is to be placed. Put some glue onto the nose and place it over the ends of the whiskers. Tape a piece of elastic to each side of the mask on the wrong side. Finally, peel the backing off the plastic and stick it to the underside of the mask.

Cut another strip of material 2 by 3½ inches (5 by 9cm). Fold the long edges in to meet at the back and glue them down. Wrap this piece around the middle of the tube and sew it in place at the back, folding in the raw edges to hide them. Sew on shirr for wearing the bow.

# PARTY & TABLE DECORATIONS

Hang this traditional wreath on the front door to give a warm welcome to guests at Christmas. To begin, take a wire coathanger and pull it into a circle. Bend the hook down to form a loop.

This Christmas wreath is based on a child's plastic hoop, and makes a delightful decoration for the wall or mantelpiece. First of all you need a plastic hoop; any size will do. Cut long strips of batting and wind them around the hoop, holding the edges in place with sticky tape. This one has two layers of medium-weight batting.

Now wire together small bunches of holly, spruce, and other foliage. Then attach each bunch to the circle. Be careful when handling the holly; you can get a bit scratched, and some people can come out in a rash from it. Keep going in one direction until the whole circle is covered.

Next take some ribbon 3 inches (8cm) wide and wind it firmly around the hoop, in the opposite direction to the batting. Make sure the batting is entirely covered. Take a contrasting ribbon, about 2 inches (6cm) wide, and wrap it over the first ribbon, leaving equal spaces between the loops. Repeat with a third ribbon, 1½ inches (4cm) wide.

On top of this add some wired pine cones and, for extra color, some curly red ribbon. (Use curling giftwrap ribbon for this, running the blunt edge of a pair of scissors along it to make it curl.) Red holly berries look great if you can get hold of them, but they tend to drop very quickly and need replacing often. Finish off with a big red satin bow.

Make sure each ribbon starts and finishes in the same place so that all the joins are together. This will be the top of the hoop. Wind tinsel around the hoop, over the ribbons. Pin or staple a wide piece of ribbon over all the joins at the top. Tape a cluster of ribbon, tinsel, baubles, and bells at the top and add a large bow to finish off.

Add several sprigs of holly, again securing them with wire. If the holly is a bit short of berries, you can add some fake berries at this point.

To hang the wreath, you will need two lengths of satin ribbon. Each piece should be twice the length of the drop from the ceiling to your hanging height, plus an extra 8 inches (20cm) for tying around the wreath. Tie each of the four ends opposite one another around the wreath so that the two lengths cross in the center.

Make four bows from the same color ribbon and pin them to the wreath over the four tying-on points.

Gently push a length of florist's wire through each of four red wax candles, approximately ½ inch (1.5cm) above the bases, as shown.

Position each candle halfway between two bows, and twist the wire around the wreath to hold it in place. To hang the wreath, tie another length of ribbon around the two main ribbons where they cross. Then make a loop to go over the hook, and tie the ends in a bow.

This festive wreath is ideal if you're short of space on the table – it can be suspended from a hook screwed into the ceiling. Use wire cutters to snip the hook off a coat hanger. Bend the hanger into a circular shape. Bunch damp bog moss around the wire to a thickness of about 2 inches (5cm), using gardener's wire around it to hold it in place.

Take several bushy branches of evergreen, such as cypress, and arrange them to cover the circlet of moss, overlapping the pieces to cover any stalks. Tie the branches to the ring with gardener's twine or wire.

A large foil star like this can hang in the center of the ceiling or over the fireplace. Try it out on a piece of plain paper first, as it is a little fiddly. Cut a piece of foil paper about 18 inches (45cm) square. Fold it in half from corner to corner, then in half twice again, making a small triangle.

Bend the single-fold edge over to the edge with three folds. Open it out, and rule two lines from the corners at the base of the triangle to the center crease. Cut along these two lines.

Refold the crease and rule two more lines, forming a small triangle as seen here. Cut this out. Now snip the point off and open the star out. Glue it to another piece of thicker foil paper for backing. Cut the star out carefully when the glue has dried. Finish it off with a ribbon rosette in the center.

This simple star can be hung on the wall or from the ceiling. First make the pattern for the star. Using a ruler and protractor, draw an equilateral triangle (each angle is 60°). Cut out the triangle and use it as a pattern to make another one. Then glue one triangle over the other to form the star. Use this pattern to cut a star from foil giftwrap.

Fold the star in half three times between opposite points. Next fold it in half three times between opposite angles as shown. Every angle and point should now have a fold in it.

The star will now easily bend into its sculptured shape. Make a small hole in its top point with a hole punch or a skewer, then put some thread through the hole to hang it up.

This decoration can be made with tissue paper, colored aluminum foil, thin cardboard, or construction paper. Cut between six and twelve bell shapes (depending on the thickness of the paper you use). Fold each shape in half and then open it out again.

Lay the cut-outs carefully on top of each other with all the creases in the center. Now take a needle and thread, and starting at the top, make three long stitches down the middle. Bring the needle up and over the bottom to secure the shapes in place. Next, make a small stitch between each long stitch. At the top, knot the two ends together.

Ease the bell open, piece by piece, until it forms a rounded shape. You could easily do exactly the same thing with other shapes such as a heart, ball, or tree.

Make these shiny decorations from foil giftwrap. Cut out eight circles in each of the following diameters: 3½ inches (9cm), 3 inches (7.5cm) and 2¼ inches (6cm). Then from cardboard cut out four circles ¾ inches (2cm) in diameter and two circles ½ inch (1.5cm) for the centers. Fold the largest foil circles into quarters and staple four of them onto a large cardboard circle.

In the same way, staple the other four foil circles to another cardboard circle. Glue the two cardboard circles together with a string between them. Leave a long piece hanging below for the other two balls. Fluff out the edges of the foil giftwrap to make a good shape.

Now make the other two balls in the same way, using the smaller cardboard circles for the tiniest. Fix the balls to the string as you go.

What could be simpler than these crisply pleated paper fans, trimmed with curling ribbons? To begin, take a strip of printed giftwrap and pleat it crosswise as shown.

Hang these pretty net fans on the wall or on the corner of a mirror, or use them to decorate a tablecloth. They are made from strips of net about 12 inches (30cm) wide and 40 inches (1 metre) long. Cut two strips of each color and concertina-fold them crosswise, treating the two layers as one. When you have finished pleating, make a few stitches through the net at one end to hold it together.

When you have finished the folding, hold the fan together by stapling it at one end. Cut some strips of gift wrap ribbon and run them along the edge of a ruler, or over a scissors blade, so that they curl.

Sew little pearl beads or silver sequins onto the net to decorate it. Trim away any rough edges on the outside of the fan.

Slip the ends of the ribbons between the folds of the fan and staple them in place. Finish by fixing a ribbon rosette over the stapled end.

Finish off by spraying some round wooden beads with silver paint and sewing them to the center of the fan to cover the pleating.

The frame for this kite is made from garden sticks. Mark off the lengths specified, and stamp on them where you want them to break! Take one stick 24 inches (60cm) long and another 16 inches (40cm) long, and tie them together with twine so that the three upper arms are equal. Next add two top pieces, 11½ inches (28cm) long, and the two lower side pieces 18½ inches (45cm) long. Tie all these pieces in place.

Now take two large sheets of brightly colored tissue paper. Tear one in half lengthwise and lay one half over the large sheet. Lightly glue it along the edges to keep it in place. Turn the paper over. Now lay the frame over the tissue, and cut around the shape, leaving a 2 inch (5cm) border all around.

These are just as colorful as real balloons, but they won't pop, or even gently expire! Cut out balloon shapes from colored cardboard or stiff paper, then cover them on one side with spray-on glitter.

Apply glue to the outside frame of the kite, and fold the edges of the tissue over it. Finish by adding a red rosette and a paper ribbon tail with bows strung along it. After use on the big day, this can be transferred to the wall of the children's room. It has to be handled carefully, but once hung up will last for ages.

Two balloon shapes can be glued together at the edges, or they can all be strung up separately. Tape the balloons to a length of colorful striped ribbon.

Lastly, use more of the same ribbon to make up some bows, and fix them to the balloons with some double-sided tape.

All you really need for this decoration is some garden wire, a little bit of tinsel, and a couple of baubles, but a pair of pliers will make it easier to manipulate the wire. Bend the wire into the shape of a bell. (You could, of course, try much more complicated shapes once you get the hang of it.)

To make these luscious lips, you will need a piece of fluorescent pink craft paper 30 by 5 inches (76 by 12.5cm). You should be able to get four strips this size out of a standard sheet of craft paper. Draw a lips shape (using folded paper will ensure symmetry) and cut it out in cardboard.

Now just wind tinsel around the wire until it is completely covered. A couple of layers will be sufficient.

Fold the paper in half from right to left, and then from right to left again. This will give you four sets of lips. Place the pattern on top and draw round it, making sure that the pattern meets each side; otherwise the lips won't hold together.

Finish off with a bauble, tied on to represent the clapper, and some bright red ribbon to tie the bells together.

Cut out the shape using sharp scissors. Join each set of lips together at the ends to make one long garland.

This makes an ideal Christmas wall hanging, particularly if you haven't room for a real tree. First make a paper pattern of a tree, about 30 inches (75cm) high and 23½ inches (59cm) wide at the widest point across the bottom branches. Also cut a pattern for the pot, about 10 inches (25cm) high. Make it about as wide as the base of the tree, with a slightly wider, 3 inch (8cm) deep "rim" at the top as shown.

Cut out two pieces of green felt from the tree pattern and two pieces of red for the pot. Also cut out a piece of batting for each. The batting for the pot should be about 1¾ inches (4.5cm) shorter, since the rim of the pot will be turned down. On the front of the tree mark diagonal lines for the branches as shown.

Place the tree pieces together, with batting on top. Pin and baste, then stitch ⅜ inch (1cm) from the edge, leaving the lower edge open. Clip the corners and turn the tree right side out. Stitch along the marked lines. Make up the pot, sewing up to 1½ inches (4cm) from the top. Turn it right side out and slip the tree inside; sew it in place. Sew the upper sides of the pot together and turn the rim down.

To decorate the tree, cut out little pockets of red felt and sew them in place as shown. Insert little gifts – either real ones or giftwrapped cardboard squares.

Finish off by adding plenty of ribbons and bells. Curtain rings also look good covered in ribbon and sewn on. Sew a loop to the top of the tree to hang it by.

This unusual decoration adds a festive touch to a mirror or favorite painting. Make it in separate sections, one to be horizontal, the other vertical. You need fake ivy, fern, and other foliage, plus pine cones, gold baubles, and gold curling giftwrap ribbon. Cut off the long stems and wire everything up as shown, using florists' wire.

Hanging up your Christmas cards always poses a problem. Here is a simple way to overcome it while making an interesting "picture" for your wall at the same time. First take a piece of wooden garden trellis and extend it. Spray it with gold paint.

For the top section gradually lay pieces on top of one another, binding the wires and stems together with tape as you go along. The arrangement should be relatively long and narrow.

While the trellis is drying, lay out some regular wooden clothes pegs and spray them gold as well. You will have to turn them over a few times so that all sides are covered.

For the second section, use the same technique, but make the arrangement fuller. Hold the two pieces as you would like them to sit on the frame, and wire them together. Bend the stem wires back so that they will slip over the frame and hold the arrangement in place.

When the trellis is dry, take some thick strands of tinsel and wind them all around the edge of the trellis to make a frame. Now hang the trellis on the wall, and use the pegs to attach the Christmas cards as they arrive.

If the day outside is gloomy, try brightening the outlook with some "stained glass window" pictures. These are cut from black art paper and backed with colored tissue. First cut out pieces of art paper 15 by 12 inches (38 by 30cm). Mark a 1½ inch (3.5cm) border all the way round. Now draw your design, taking care that it is always connected in some way to the outer border.

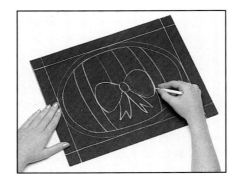

You can always have snow at Christmas, even when the sun is shining outside. Make this snow-flake in foil or in plain white paper and hang it over a windowpane. First take a square of paper and fold it into quarters, then in half diagonally, then lastly back on itself as shown.

Next cut away any parts of the picture that you want to be colored, taking care not to detach the black areas from the frame.

Make a pattern of the chosen design, then mark it on the folded paper with a black felt-tip pen. Shade the areas that are to be cut away, then cut them out. Open out the snowflake. If you use very flimsy aluminum foil, glue the snowflake onto a piece of paper, and cut out around it. This will make it easier to hang.

Now glue tissue paper to the back. For your first attempt use just one color; then as you feel more confident, you can build up pictures using three or more different colored tissues. When the picture is finished, affix it lightly to the windowpane, then watch what happens when the light shines through.

Finally, decorate the snowflake with lots of sequins in bright jewel colors.

This mobile is made from cardboard (or construction paper) bird shapes with tissue paper fanned wings and tails. For each bird cut two bird shapes, using the template on page 246. Glue the two pieces together, placing thread between them, in line with the wings, to hang the bird from. Mark where the wings will fit, and cut a slit.

For the fanned wings take a piece of tissue paper 14 by 9 inches (35 by 22cm) and concertina-fold it lengthwise. Round off the edges and push the folded paper through the slit in the bird, so that there is an equal amount on each side. Glue the inside edges upward to the sides of the bird to make the wings fan out.

These little fluffy chicks make a charming mobile. For each chick you need two pompons (see page 19 for instructions). For the larger pompon use cardboard circles, 2½ inches (6cm) in diameter with 1 inch (2.5cm) holes. The small circles are 2 inches (5cm) across with the same size hole. When the larger one is ready to be cut away, put a pipe cleaner through the hole to form the legs and feet.

Now cut and tie the pompons, joining the head and body together by tying the spare yarn tightly. Make one or two stitches through the head and body to hold them in place.

For the tail use a piece of tissue paper 14 by 5 inches (35 by 12cm), and concertina-fold it widthwise. Round off the edges, then slip one end over the tail of the cardboard bird; glue it in place as shown. Finish off with sequins for the eyes. Hang the birds from two crossed sticks, tied or glued together.

Trim each chick with a felt beak, eyes, and wings, plus a feather for the tail, sticking them on with a dab of glue. Tie a piece of shirr around the neck, and use this to attach a piece of rickrack or ribbon to the chick. Then hang it onto two crossed sticks, tied together. Glue the rickrack in place to prevent the chicks from slipping off.

# HEART STRINGS

For this mobile cut out 40 hearts in thin pink cardboard and 40 in blue. Glue one side of the blue heart. Lay the end of a long piece of nylon thread on it, then place a pink heart on top; press them firmly together. Now glue another two hearts together, with the thread between them, leaving a gap of about 1½ inches (4cm) between this and the first heart.

Add three more hearts to the thread. Cut off the thread about 8 inches (20cm) above the top heart. Make seven more heart strings. Cut two circles of cardboard using a dessert plate as a pattern. In one make eight tiny holes, about 1 inch (2.5cm) from the edge. Insert the strings and tape them in place. In the other circle insert four threads and tie them to a curtain ring. Glue the two circles together.

# SWAYING PALMS

This tropical-style mobile is made of colored modeling clay, the kind you can bake. You simply mold it and bake it in the oven. Then glue the pieces together and varnish it for a lovely shiny finish. You need eight palm trees for the mobile. Roll out the clay with a rolling pin and cut out the shape of the tree using the template on page 246.

If using more than one color, cut the trunk and branches separately. Remember to make a hole in the top to hang each one. Also cut out a ring of clay about 6 inches (15cm) in diameter, with eight holes on the outer edge and four on the inner. Bake the shapes as instructed. When they are cool, glue the trunks and branches together. Varnish them on both sides.

To string them, use a strong nylon or wax cord. The first should be 2 inches (5cm) long, the second 4 inches (10cm) and so on, with 2 inches (5cm) added to each length. This will give the impression that the trees fall in a spiral. Slip them through the holes in the support and knot them onto a bead above. Knot four more strings through the inner edge, and attach them to a ring to hang the mobile.

These decorations are made from a basic recipe of 2 cups (250g) all-purpose flour, ½ cup (125g) butter, ⅔ cup (150g) superfine sugar, and 2 egg yolks. Cream the butter and sugar until fluffy. Then add the egg yolks and flour, and mix them into a firm dough. Roll the dough out until it is about ½ inch (1cm) thick, and cut out the chosen shapes.

Skewer a hole in each, so that you can push a thread through later. (This may close up during baking – in which case you will have to pierce another hole in them when they are cold – but very carefully, as the cookies have a habit of breaking!) Put them onto a greased baking sheet, and bake them at 350°F for 15 minutes.

When the cookies are cool, make up some fairly stiff frosting using confectioner's sugar and water, and decorate them. Thread them onto some wax thread – or ribbon if the hole is big enough – and hang them on the tree straight away; they won't stay there very long!

These ornaments are very easy to make; all you need are some bells from last year's tree. If you haven't got any, look for suitable molds in the cake decorating section of a department store. Put a few spoonfuls of granulated sugar in a dish, and moisten it with food coloring.

When the coloring is thoroughly mixed in, push the sugar into a bell mold, pressing it in firmly to fill the entire cavity.

Now simply tap the sugar bell out of the mold. Leave the bells to dry out overnight. To hang them on the tree, cut out a little tissue paper flower. Thread a loop through it and glue it to the top of the bell. (These ornaments are not edible, and should be placed out of the reach of small children.)

These little boxes make charming tree decorations. If you haven't got any suitable ones that you can wrap for the tree, you can easily make your own from cardboard. For a cube, you need to mark out a Latin cross shape. The lower arm of the cross should be twice as long as the top and side arms. Also add a ½ inch (1.5cm) border to all arms except the top one for gluing the cube together.

Fold along all the lines as shown. Then bring the cube together, gluing all the sides in place.

Now simply wrap the box in attractive paper, and tie it with ribbons and bows to look like a package. Pop it on or under the tree.

These pretty ornaments can be made any size. For a cube shape the pattern is a Latin cross (as shown), the long piece being twice the length of the others; all the other sides must be of equal length. Cut this shape out in satin, then cut out a piece of iron-on facing, ½ inch (1cm) smaller all round. Iron on the facing. Also iron in creases to form the sides of the cube.

Placing the right sides together, sew all the seams. Use a small running stitch, cutting into the corners and using the edge of the facing as a seamline.

Leave one edge open and then turn the cube the right side out. Stuff it with polyester batting, then slipstitch the opening edges together. Decorate the cube with ribbon and bows and set it on a branch of your Christmas tree. For a rectangular box, simply widen the long section of the cross. The round box is a purchased box with satin glued onto it.

Another fun tree decoration that will last from year to year. Cut out the tree and pot in cardboard, using the templates on page 246. Now cut the shapes out in two different colors of felt, cutting two each of tree and pot. Place the two tree shapes together, and work a buttonhole stitch around the edges, leaving the trunk end open.

Stuff the tree lightly with a little batting. Now buttonhole stitch around the pot, leaving the top open. Slip the trunk into the pot, and then lightly stuff the pot. Sew the tree and pot together at the sides.

These jolly Santa faces will add Christmas cheer to the tree. Cut out all the pieces in felt, using the template on page 246. Glue the main face piece onto a piece of cardboard. When it is dry, cut around it.

Sew a little bow to the top of the pot, and decorate the tree with sequins and tinsel. Fix some gold or silver thread under the star on the top of the tree, so you can hang it up.

All you have to do now is glue on all the other pieces. The nose and cheeks are affixed before the mustache, which goes on top.

Place a loop of thread under the circle on the top of the hat, to hang up the face. Glue on two dark sequins to represent the eyes.

Make a pattern for a Christmas stocking using the template on page 246. Cut it out double in one piece by placing the pattern on the fold of the felt. Cut a strip of fake fur to fit the stocking, about 2 inches (5cm) deep. Catch the fur to the felt, top and bottom, by hand, with small stitches.

Now overcast the two sides of the stocking together, starting at the ankle and working around the foot and up the front. Turn the stocking the right side out.

These miniature crackers can be hung on the Christmas tree or on the wall. First take a piece of drawing paper or light cardboard about 3 inches (7.5cm) wide and long enough to roll into a tube. Hold it together with a little sticky tape.

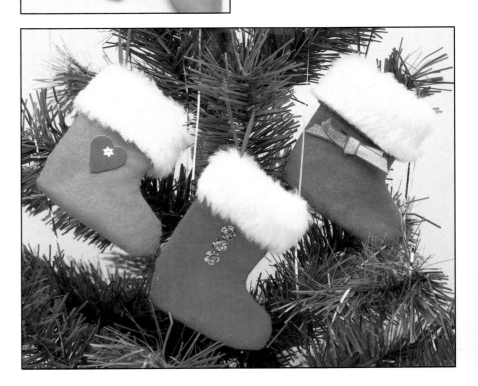

Turn the fur down about 1 inch (2.5cm) to the right side, catching it down around the edge. Decorate the stocking with sequins, bows, etc., and sew a loop of ribbon just inside the edge to hang it from the tree.

Cut a piece of crêpe paper or aluminum foil twice as long as the tube, and roll the tube in it. Stick the edges together with double-sided tape. Squeeze the paper together at both ends, and tie some thread around them. Fluff out the ends and make small cuts in them to make a fringe.

To decorate the cracker, cut some extra, narrow pieces of crêpe paper or aluminum foil. Fringe them at the edges and wrap them around the tube as before. Alternatively, tie a bow round the cracker or stick a silver star in the middle. To the ends tie a length of ribbon or sparkly twine by which to hang the cracker.

Here is another cute tree decoration that is fun to make: tiny Christmas puddings. You start with regular Ping-pong balls. Spear each one onto a fine knitting pin and paint it brown. After two or three coats, for a dark rich color, finish off with a clear varnish to give the "puddings" a lovely shine.

By the time Christmas arrives, you may not have much extra cash for Christmas tree baubles, so these colorful fakes are a great way of economizing. First cut some circles, with a little loop on the top, from some lightweight cardboard. Now mark out a pattern on each in pencil. Simple zigzags and curved lines are effective, but not too complicated to fill in.

Now take some modeling clay, the sort you can bake in the oven, and roll it into a ball, the same size as the Ping-pong balls. Over this, mold a thick circle of white clay, to look like custard sauce. Bake this in the oven, and then remove it from the clay ball immediately. Pop it onto a pudding, so that it fits as it cools down and hardens. Don't forget to poke a hole in the top at this point.

Paint each bauble with several different colors, waiting for each to dry before painting the next. If you have some gold or silver paint, make good use of this, as it is very effective. Use black to make definite lines between colors.

When the clay is cold, glue it to the "pudding." Now take a double thread, knot the end and thread it through the pudding from the bottom upward. Trim off the ends, then finish each "pudding" by gluing on foil holly leaves and red bead berries.

When the baubles are dry, attach some thread, ribbon, or some tinsel wire, so that you can hang them up.

If you haven't any shiny bells for the Christmas tree, it's not difficult to make some from foil, beads, and a little string. First take a saucer and mark around it onto the back of some colored foil paper. Cut out the circle, then fold it in half, and cut along the fold line. Fold each half of the circle into a cone and glue it in place.

For the clapper, string a bead onto a length of thread — preferably waxed — and tie a knot over the bead. Lay the thread against the bell so that the clapper is at the right level, then tie a knot level with the hole in the top. This prevents the string from being pulled through the hole when threaded. Pull the string through the hole from the inside. Thread on a smaller bead at the top and knot in place.

Finish each bell by dabbing a little glue around the bottom edge and sprinkling on some glitter. When you have made three bells, string them together, and attach them to a ring so that they can be hung on the tree. Wind a little tinsel wire around the string, and tie a couple of bows for that final touch of glamour.

These miniature lanterns make attractive Christmas tree ornaments. First take a piece of foil-covered paper 5½ inches (11cm) square. Fold it in half, and rule a line ¾ inch (1.5cm) from the loose edges. Now rule lines ½ inch (1cm) apart, from the fold up to this first line. Cut along these lines and open out the sheet of paper.

Hold the paper with the cuts running vertically, and glue the two sides together. When this is firm, set the lantern on the table and gently push the top down to make the sides poke outward.

Finally, cut a strip of matching paper 5 inches (13cm) long and ½ inch (1cm) wide. Dab some glue on each end, and glue the strip onto the inside of the lantern, at the top, for a handle.

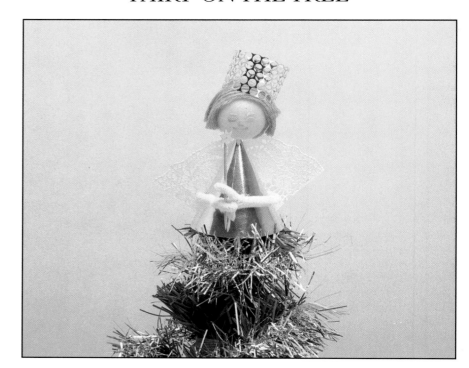

A shiny foil star makes a striking decoration for the top of the Christmas tree. Using the instructions on page 98, cut out a pattern in cardboard. Now cut two squares of cardboard, slightly larger than the star template. Cover each side with a different colored foil. Next cut out two stars, one from each foil-covered squares.

This traditional English Christmas tree-top decoration makes a charming addition to the festivities. Using a saucer, cut a circle out of silver foil paper. Cut the circle in half and fold one half into a cone, tapping it in place.

Take a ruler and pencil, and placing the ruler between two opposite points, mark a line on each star from one point to the center. Cut along these lines and then simply slot the two stars together.

Take a pink pipe cleaner and tape it to the back of the cone; then bend it into arms and hands. On top of this fix a triangle of doily to represent wings, using double-sided tape. For the head, take a regular table tennis ball and skewer it onto a wooden pick. Push the pick into the cone.

Use sticky tape and hold the points together, then attach a piece of green garden wire to one set of points. You can then use the wire to attach the star to the tree. Finish the star by dabbing some glue onto the points and sprinkling glitter over them for an extra-sparkly effect.

The hair is made from gray crewel or yarn, stuck on with double-sided tape. The crown is a small piece of silver sequin waste. Draw the facial features with a fine-tipped silver pen. For the wand, spray a pick with silver paint and stick a small silver star on one end.

This sort of arrangement always looks very hard to achieve, but in fact it is very simple, provided you assemble everything you need before starting. What you need is a ring of florists' foam with a plastic base, which you can get from a florist. Also buy three plastic candle holders; stick these into the foam.

Believe it or not, this arrangement is quite simple once you get the hang of folding the cones. You need two colors of foil paper. Cut out lots of boat shapes 6½ inches (16.5cm) along the top and 5 inches (12.5cm) along the bottom and about 2½ inches (6cm) deep. Glue one color to another, back-to-back.

You will need holly, ivy, and fern, all of them either real or fake, plus a selection of dried flowers. Daisy-like sunrays, yellow strawflowers or everlasting flowers, yarrow, safflowers, and sea lavender are used here. Simply break pieces off these and stick them into the foam. Try to space the flowers evenly in between the foliage.

Form each boat into a cone and glue it in place. The first few you make may not look too professional, but it doesn't matter – these can go on the outside of the stand and will be partially covered. You will soon get the hang of folding the cones. Bend the bottoms under; it helps to hold the shape and looks tidier.

When you have finished, stick three candles into the holders already placed. If any of the foliage is real, make sure you keep the foam damp.

When you have made several cones, start gluing them around the edge of a 8-inch (20-cm) diameter silver cake board. Place another two layers inside the first, leaving room for a chunky candle in the middle.

# RIBBONS AND CURLS

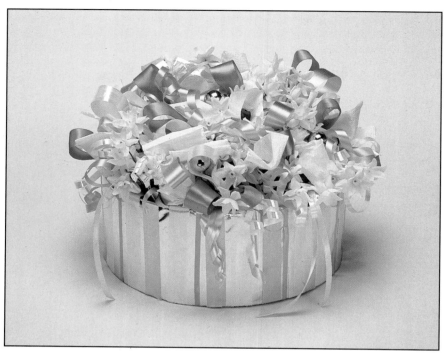

W hat could be prettier than this profusion of ribbons and flowers? The one shown is pink and white, but you should choose whatever matches your décor. First of all you will need a cookie or cake tin, Cover the outside with silver foil paper, allowing a little extra at the top to turn over and glue. (This will be easier if you snip down to the tin.) Decorate it with strips of ribbon.

Take a block of florists' foam and cut it to fit inside the tin, using the extra bits to fill in the gaps around it.

Now wire up pieces of giftwrap ribbon, little baubles, strips of crêpe paper, and silk flowers. Curl the ribbon by running the blunt edge of a pair of scissors along it. Push the wires into the foam, arranging them until the tin is totally full. Use strips of ribbon around the outside, and let them fall over the side of the tin.

# FOREST FOLIAGE

T he sideboard, as well as the table, needs a little dressing up at Christmas. This is bright and cheery, and the materials are quite easy to find. If you don't have woodland nearby, your florist should have small sections of bark for sale. Also buy a plastic candle holder. First put a large lump of green modeling clay onto the bark, and stick your candle holder on the top.

Now take some plastic or silk fern and spray it gold. Break off pieces when it is dry, and stick them into the modeling clay. Also wire up strands of red paper ribbon, pine cones, and red baubles and stick these in.

When the modeling clay is artistically concealed, place a red candle in the holder, and set the arrangement on the sideboard. Put a mat under it, though, or it may scratch the surface.

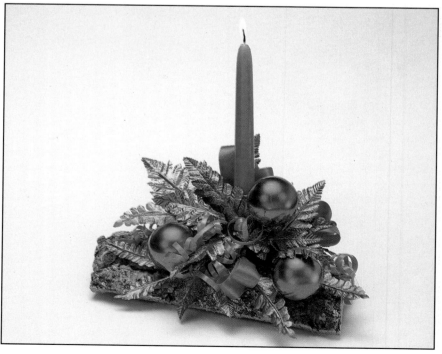

Spring is in the air, with a shiny silver pot plant, blossoming with pink silk flowers. You need a small plastic pot and a small, graceful tree branch. Spray them both with silver paint.

Now take a block of modeling clay, weighting the base with a stone if necessary. Push the silver branch into the middle and fix the modeling clay into the pot. For the "earth" scrunch up a piece of aluminum foil and arrange it around the branch.

For the blossoms you need little pink silk flowers, scrunched up pink tissue, green tissue leaves, and pink and green giftwrap ribbon. Glue these along the branch as shown, spacing them so as to look reasonably realistic.

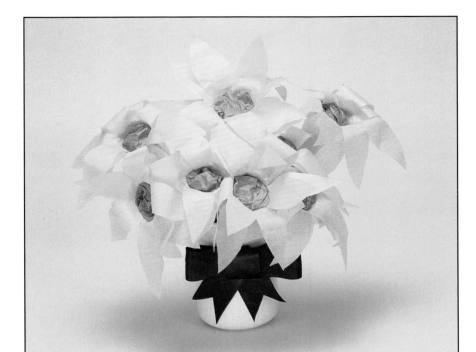

Make some spring flowers that will bloom throughout the year. For the base of each daffodil head, cut a section from an egg box and trim it down to an even edge. Use a yellow one if you can, or else paint it yellow. Next take a flexible paper or plastic straw and roll it in a strip of green tissue, gluing both long and edges. Trim the ends and bend the straw without tearing the paper.

Cut out some yellow tissue petals and glue first one row, then a second, around the inside of the egg box base.

Finally, scrunch up a small piece of orange tissue paper and glue it to the center of the flower.

If you have no room for a proper Christmas tree, this would be a good alternative – small but spectacular. First take a medium-size plastic flower pot, about 6 inches (15cm) in diameter. Fill it, up to about 1 inch (2.5cm) from the rim, with fast-drying cement or wood putty. When this is just setting, insert a piece of ½ inch (1.5cm) dowelling about 16 inches (40cm) long.

When the putty is dry, spray paint the pot, the dowel, and the "earth's" surface gold. Lay it down to spray it, and when one side is dry, roll it over and spray the other side. The whole thing – especially the pot – will need a couple of coats.

When the paint is dry, take a ball of florists' foam at least 5 inches (12cm) in diameter and push it on top of the dowelling.

Now take short lengths of deep red and green satin ribbon, gold ribbon, shiny baubles, and gold tinsel. Wire them all up, ready to push into the foam. Start with about a dozen of each; you can add to them as you go along, if necessary.

Start inserting the wires into the sphere, arranging the ribbons and baubles until it is covered, with no foam showing through. Finally, wire up some curling giftwrap ribbon and insert it into the bottom of the ball. (Curl the ribbon by running the blunt edge of a pair of scissors along it.) Wind gold tinsel around the "trunk" of the tree, and tie a large bow around the pot as a finishing touch.

These small fir trees are fun to decorate and add a festive touch to any Christmas sideboard or buffet table. For the gold tree, make small bows of fine gold ribbon. Drape a string of gold beads in a spiral over the tree, starting at the top. Fix the bows in between the loops of beads.

Wrap some plaid ribbon around the pot and secure the ends with fabric glue. Make a separate bow and attach it with glue or pins.

For the red tree, cut fine ribbon into 6 inch (15cm) lengths. Tie them into bows and position them on the tree as shown.

Tie some tiny red ornaments to the branches; or, if the tree is dense enough, simply place them in the spaces between the bows. Add a wide red ribbon sash around the terra cotta pot, tying it in a big bow.

A mound of luscious apricots, flowers, and leaves makes a pretty centerpiece for a summer buffet or dinner party. Place a white doily on a glass or china cake stand. Carefully push ivy leaves underneath the edge of the doily. The leaves should be washed and can be wiped with cooking oil for extra shine.

Holding the doily in place with one hand, arrange the apricots in a pile. (If the apricots are to be eaten, do not let them touch the ivy leaves, which are poisonous.) Then arrange a few sprays of cream-colored freesias around the pile of apricots.

Finally, slot flowers into the gaps between the apricots – any small cream or white flowers will do; those used here are narcissi. Check with your florist that the flowers you choose are not poisonous.

For an unusual Easter centerpiece fill a rustic basket with a selection of different eggs. The basket shown contains a mixture of hen's eggs, tiny speckled quail's eggs (which can be eaten as an hors d'oeuvre), and carved wooden eggs. Half fill the basket with paper to form a base for the eggs, then add a layer of packing straw.

Arrange your selection of eggs in the packing straw to show off their different colors and patterns. Tie a ribbon around the handle of the basket to provide a finishing touch.

# TULIP CANDLESTICKS

# FALL GOLD

A touch of gold gives this platter of fruit and nuts extra richness. Begin by spraying ivy, clementines, bay leaves, and fir cones with gold paint. (If the fruit will be eaten make sure that the paint you are using is nontoxic.)

Place the ivy leaves around the edge of a plain oval platter. The flatter the plate, the better, for this will let the ivy leaves to hang over the edge.

A simple motif such as a tulip can add style to the plainest of candlesticks. For this design you will need a pair of pink candlesticks, a fine paint brush, and some garnet red and green ceramic paints. Decorate the top first, firmly holding the candlestick by the stem as you do so. Begin by painting the red flowers and clusters of tiny red dots, then fill in with green foliage.

Paint the stem and finally the base of the candlestick after the top has dried. Finish with lines of tiny red dots at the top and bottom of the stem, following the shape of the candlestick. Finally, when the paint is completely dry, apply a coat of ceramic varnish.

Arrange the clementines on the platter and surround them with dates and nuts. Place a bunch of shiny black grapes on top. Add the gold leaves and fir cones for a luxurious finishing touch.

# FROSTED FRUIT

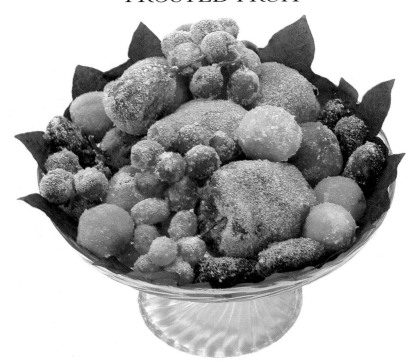

This stunning centerpiece looks grand enough to grace the most formal dinner party, and yet is very simple to make. Using a pastry brush, coat each piece of fruit with egg white.

Working over a large plate, sprinkle sugar over the fruit so that it adheres to the coating of egg. Alternatively, the fruit can be dipped into a bowl of sugar, although this tends to make the sugar lumpy.

Ivy leaves are used here to form a decorative border; but remember to use a doily to separate the poisonous leaves from the fruit if you intend to eat the fruit later.

# IVY CANDLE-RING

This elegant candle-ring is the ideal centerpiece for a special dinner party at any time of the year. A circular cake base serves as the foundation for the arrangement. Begin by attaching strands of ivy to the edge of the base, securing them with thumbtacks.

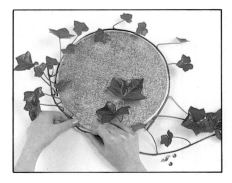

Build up the ring by adding more strands and bunches of leaves until only a small space remains in the center. Push stems of freesia among the ivy leaves to provide color contrast.

Use a mixture of white and green candles of varying heights to form the center of the arrangement. Secure each candle to the base with a blob of glue or modeling clay.

## NEW YEAR'S CENTERPIECE

For a bright party centerpiece – ideal for New Year's – fill a glass bowl with a mixture of shiny glass baubles, foil crackers, feathers, and streamers. To make clusters of small baubles, first remove the hanging string. Put a dab of glue inside the neck of each bauble and push in a short length of florists' wire. Leave them to dry.

Hold the wired baubles in a cluster and wind fine fuse wire around the stems to hold them together.

Wrap a piece of shiny giftwrap ribbon around the stems and tie it into a bow. Arrange the baubles and other ornaments in the bowl as shown.

## FLOWERS AND FRILLS

This pretty centerpiece is a good wintertime alternative to a vase of real flowers. Lay a sheet of colored tissue between two different-colored layers of net. Place a vase in the center of the net and tissue, and gather the three layers up around the neck of the vase.

Secure the net and tissue in place with a piece of twine or an elastic band. Tie a length of contrasting wide satin ribbon in a bow around the neck of the vase.

Fluff out the layers of net and tissue to create a frilled effect. Fill the vase with artificial flowers – such as the tulips shown here – or with real flowers, if you prefer.

These individual cakes, each with its own candle, make an unusual alternative to a large birthday cake for a children's party. They also form an attractive centerpiece. Decorate each cake with a pattern, or pipe a child's name onto it.

Stick a long taper candle into each cake and arrange the cakes on a large plate. Once lit, the candles should not be left to burn for too long, as the hot wax will begin to drop onto the cakes.

Exquisite marzipan fruits deserve special presentation. Nestling in little tissue "packages" and piled into a cake stand, they make a colorful centerpiece. All you need is several different colors of tissue paper and some pinking shears. Instead of marzipan fruits, you could use chocolates or marrons glacés.

From a double layer of one color of tissue, cut a 4 inch (10cm) square. Pinking shears give an attractive serrated edge. From another color of tissue, also double, cut a smaller square, measuring about 2½ inches (6cm).

Lay the smaller square on top of the larger one. Place the marzipan fruit in the center and gather the tissue around it. Hold it in place for a few seconds and then let go; the crumpled tissue will retain its rosette shape. Place several of the packages on a doily-lined glass or china cake stand.

For a summer table centerpiece nothing can surpass the beauty of flowers. The secret of successful flower arranging is a careful choice of containers and a harmonious color scheme. When using several containers, try to get a variety of shapes. The pitchers used here have contrasting forms but similar colors; the flowers include shades of pink, white, and red.

The tall pitcher contains a mixture of windflowrs ranunculus, kaffir lily (*schizostylis*), and white asters, the mixture of shapes providing variety. The smallest pitcher contains a tiny narcissi, ranunculus, and anemones, with a few sprigs of love-in-a-mist (*nigella*). The deep red windflower at the front serves as a focal point.

This fat, rounded pitcher has a fairly wide neck and is therefore ideal for full-blown roses, which look good clustered together to form a close, rounded shape. Delicate stalks of white aster and a few heads of love-in-a-mist show up well against the pale pink roses and give more definition to the arrangement.

Although flowers are most often arranged in vases, it is just as easy to create a pretty centerpiece using other containers you may have around the house. This natural, yet graceful, arrangement uses a mixture of spring flowers in jam jars. A few colored glass bottles are added for contrast.

Here a squat clear jar is used for a mixture of white flowers and silvery-green foliage, forming a cool two-color arrangement.

A single hyacinth is enough to fill the smaller jar, and the twisted stem of a windflower fits perfectly into a narrow blue glass bottle. A colorful bunch of windflowers in another jam jar completes the centerpiece.

This cute little rabbit can be popped over a soft-cooked egg to keep it warm. First cut out two rabbit shapes in white felt, using the template on page 246. Cut the ears from pink felt, the vest from yellow, and the nose and eyes from black. Glue them in place. Embroider the mouth and whiskers in black thread. Glue on sequins for the buttons and for the whites of eyes.

Take a piece of ribbon 2 inches (5cm) long and glue the ends together to form a loop. Tie a piece of thread tightly around the middle of the ribbon to form a bow. Sew it to the rabbit between the mouth and the top of the vest.

With wrong sides facing, sew the front and back together along the edge, using blanket stitch.

To break the ice at a kids' party – iced cupcake name badges. The template for the pieces is on page 246. Cut each cake shape from thin cardboard as a base for the felt. Then cut out the top and bottom pieces, again in cardboard.

Glue the latter pieces to different colors of felt and cut around them. Now glue these separate pieces to the base card.

Finish off by sticking a name label to the front of the bun and a little double-sided tape to the back. When the little guests arrive, simply tear off the backing from the tape and label them!

W hy not decorate a plain white tablecloth with a placemat outline to match your china? All you need is a raw potato and some paint. First cut the potato into a cube about the size of your chosen motif. The leaf shape shown here is about 1½ inches (3cm) square. Using a sharp knife, cut the motif on one side of the cube as shown.

T his pretty tablecloth isn't hard to make, but it requires a bit of patience. You can make the cloth yourself or buy one. Then buy enough ribbon in each color to run along four sides of the cloth, plus 8 inches (24cm) if using a store-bought cloth. Position the ribbons as shown, with fusible webbing underneath (omitting the area where they will cross). Pin them in place.

Use a paint suitable for fabric, or a water-based paint if you are printing on a paper tablecloth. Spread the paint evenly over the raised motif.

Continue to pin the ribbons in place along all the edges, making sure that you keep them straight. Thread the ribbons underneath one another to create a lattice effect, as shown. If you are using a store-bought cloth, let the ribbons overlap the edge by 1 inch (3cm); this will be folded under later.

On a piece of stiff paper, draw the outline of the "placemat" in black felt-tip pen. Place this under the cloth as a guide when printing. Press the potato down onto the cloth, taking care not to smudge it. Practice first on a spare piece of paper. The same technique can be used to print a border design around the edge of the napkin.

Replace the corner pins with basting stitches, if you are working on an unhemmed cloth; this provides extra stability. Press the ribbons in place with a warm iron, removing pins as you go and stopping just short of the basting. Finally, hem the edges. On a store-bought cloth, sew the ribbon ends to the wrong side by hand.

Transform a plain tablecloth with this eyecatching design. Choose a brush the correct size for your design, and use a paint suitable for fabrics. (Because the paint is applied quite thickly, a paper tablecloth is not suitable.)

Practice first on a spare piece of cloth or paper, dipping the brush into the paint for each new stroke. Then paint the cloth, applying the lighter color first; let it dry thoroughly.

Paint on the second color in broad sweeps, letting the paint fade off toward the end of each brushstroke. Follow the manufacturer's directions for fixing the fabric.

Rag-rolling, or ragging, is a quick and easy way to transform a plain fabric or paper tablecloth. Pour a water-based paint or fabric dye onto a plate, and dip a crumpled piece of cloth in it. Blot the cloth on some waste paper or fabric to remove excess paint.

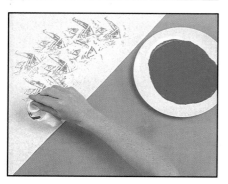

Lightly press the crumpled fabric onto a spare piece of paper or cloth to practice getting an even amount of paint over the area to be covered. Once you feel confident, rag the tablecloth, adding a second color (once the first has dried) if wished. If using fabric dye, follow the manufacturer's directions for fixing the color.

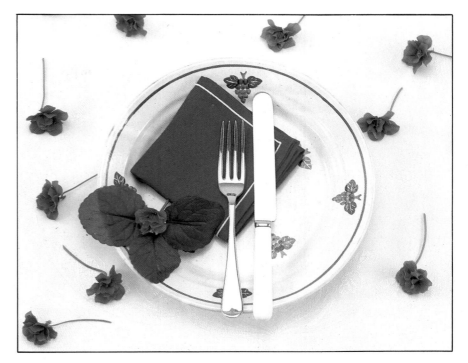

A dd a touch of luxury to a dinner party by decorating your own tablecloth in gold. First choose a simple image, such as the fleur-de-lys motif shown here. You can either decorate an existing cloth or buy a length of wide, inexpensive, cotton fabric. Draw the shape in pencil first, and then go over it in gold paint.

This simple idea can transform a plain tablecloth into something special. Choose a pure white or pastel-colored tablecloth and artificial flowers with small blossoms. You will also need some green sewing thread and a needle.

If the flowers you have chosen have several blooms to a stem, trim them into individual sprigs. Set aside the remaining leaves.

To echo the shape of the fleur-de-lys symbol, you can dress up your table napkins as shown. A napkin with a lacy edge will look best. Fold the napkin into a square. Keeping the lacy edge nearest to you, fold the left- and right-hand corners in to overlap one another. Fold the remaining point in to meet them.

Slide the napkin, lacy edge toward you, into a shining foil gift bag. Because both napkin and china are white, a lacy gold coaster was inserted into the bag underneath the lace detail on the napkin to give it more definition.

Sew the flower sprigs to the cloth. You can use as many or as few sprigs as you wish: sew one or two by each place setting or, for a stunning effect, cover the whole cloth with them – leaving room for place settings and serving dishes. Place the leftover leaves with a single flower sprig on each guest's plate.

# HARLEQUIN PLACEMAT

This unusual placemat is easily made from cardboard and a wallpaper border. A black and white border has been chosen to coordinate with the table setting on pages 96-97. Cut a 12 inch (30cm) square from a sheet of thick cardboard, using a steel rule and craft knife to ensure precision.

Cut the border into four strips, allowing a little extra on each strip for trimming. Apply double-sided tape to the back of each strip, but do not peel off the protective backing strip yet. Lay two adjacent strips in place; where they meet at the corners, try to match the pattern repeat. Holding one strip on top of the other, cut diagonally across the corner.

Holding each strip in place along its inner edge, begin to peel back the protective paper from the double-sided tape, as shown. Rub a soft cloth along the border as you peel to stick it in place.

# GO FOR GOLD

Give a touch of luxury to plain white china by using a larger gold plate underneath each dinner plate. You will need some old white china plates, about ½ to 1 inch (1.5 to 2.5cm) wider all around than your dinner plates. You will also need a few ivy leaves (at Christmas use holly and mistletoe as well), gold spray paint, and a few gold or silver dragées.

Place the plate on a large sheet of scrap paper and spray it with gold paint, making sure that you follow the manufacturer's directions on the can.

Lay the holly and ivy leaves on a sheet of scrap paper and coat them with gold paint. Leave them to dry for 10 to 15 minutes. Then arrange the painted leaves on the smaller white plate with an unsprayed sprig of mistletoe for contrast. Add a few silver dragées for the finishing touch.

# PRETTY PVC PLACEMAT

Attractive and simple to make, these PVC (vinyl) placemats will also readily wipe clean. Cut a 12 inch (30cm) square from a sheet of thick cardboard. Take the diagonal measurement of the square – 17 inches (42.5cm) for this size mat. Mark a square of that size on the wrong side of the PVC, then cut it out.

Place the cardboard square diagonally on the larger square of PVC. Spread a strong glue all over the cardboard and also on the exposed triangle of PVC. Leave them to dry until tacky.

Fold each triangle of PVC into the center of the cardboard square so that they all meet. Press them firmly in place on the surface with a soft cloth to ensure that there are no air bubbles.

# LACE-TRIMMED PLACEMAT

Delicate lace edging and pastel ribbon give a pretty, feminine look to a place setting. Use a plain white handkerchief, or hem a piece of fabric about 12 inches (30cm) square. Cut a length of lace trimming approximately 50 inches (130cm) long. Sew it around the edge of the fabric, gathering it at each corner and joining the ends neatly.

Cut four lengths of ⅜-inch (1cm-) wide ribbon and stick them down along the join with double-sided tape. (See page 132 for directions on mitering corners.)

Cut an 8 inch (20cm) length of ribbon and tie it in a bow; trim the ends neatly. Attach it to the corner of the mat with double-sided tape, or sew it on with a few stitches. The ribbon can easily be removed when the mat needs washing.

This sparkling placemat is an obvious winner for Christmas. First draw a Christmas tree on the reverse (matt) side of a piece of shiny green cardboard. The length should be about 4 inches (10cm) longer than the diameter of your dinner plate and the width about 8 inches (20cm) wider. Cut out the mat using a craft knife and a steel ruler.

Add "ornaments" by sticking tiny baubles to the tips of the tree using strong glue.

Jolly up a plastic or paper tablecloth for a children's party by using colorful strips of ribbon to mark out individual place settings. All you need, besides the tablecloth, is 50 inches (1.3m) of patterned ribbon for each setting and some double-sided tape.

Cut out or buy a star shape to put at the top of the tree. Finally, stick small silver stars over the mat. Or, if you prefer, just scatter the stars freely over the mat, first positioning each mat on the table.

For each setting draw a 12 inches (30cm) square on the tablecloth. Use a ruler and set square (right-angled triangle) for accuracy. Cut the ribbon into four equal lengths. Stick tape onto the back of each ribbon and remove the backing. Stick the ribbon onto the cloth, overlapping it at the corners as shown and smoothing it just enough to hold it in place.

Where the ribbons overlap, at the corners, lift them gently and cut diagonally across them to give you neatly mitered corners. When you have trimmed each corner, run a finger along the ribbons, sticking them firmly in place.

# COLOR-FLECKED PLACEMAT

The perfect solution if you can't find tablemats in the right color – paint your own, using plain cork tablemats and two colors of water-based paint. For applying the paint you will need an artists' paintbrush and a natural sponge.

Paint the cork mat all over with the lighter-colored paint. Leave it to dry. If the color is very pale you may need to apply a second coat.

Dip the sponge into a saucer containing the color; dab it a few times on a piece of scrap paper to remove any excess paint. Sponge the mat all over, letting the first paint color show through. When the paint is dry, apply a coat of clear polyurethane varnish for protection.

# PICNIC TRES CHIC

Convenient and also stylish, this placemat roll wraps up each person's flatware and napkin until needed. For each roll you will need a quilted cotton placemat and matching napkin, and three coordinating ribbons, about 22 inches (55cm) long.

Lay the placemat flat, wrong side up. Lay the napkin and flatware on top, then roll them up together as shown.

Trim the ends of the ribbons diagonally. Lay the roll on top of the ribbons and tie them around it into a bow.

This pretty design is not as difficult to create as it may appear. The technique is similar to that used to make the origami "fortune cookies" so popular with children. Lay the square napkin flat, and begin by folding each of the four corners into the center.

Here's a quick and simple way to dress up a plain napkin for a tea party. All you need is a square paper doily, preferably in a color contrasting with the napkin, and a floral motif. Begin by folding the napkin into a triangle.

Repeat this same procedure, drawing the corners inward to make an even smaller square. Then turn the napkin over and repeat for the third time, holding the corners down in the center to keep them in place.

Fold the doily diagonally. To create a "spine" to allow for the thickness of the napkin, unfold the doily and make another crease about ⅜ inch (1cm) from the first fold.

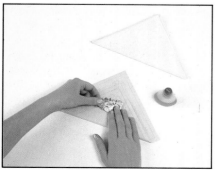

Still keeping your finger on the center, reach behind the napkin to one of the corners tucked underneath. Draw this gently outward as shown until it peaks out beyond the corner of the square. Repeat the process with all four flaps to form the petals. Finally, reaching underneath again, pull out the four single flaps to make the sepals.

Cut out a Victorian scrap or other floral motif and glue it to the center of the small (top) side of the doily. Insert the napkin.

# PURE AND SIMPLE

This elegant napkin fold is easier to produce than it looks. First fold the napkin in half diagonally. Then bring the left- and right-hand corners up to meet at the apex.

Turn the napkin over, and fold the lower corner up slightly as shown.

Fold the left- and right-hand corners underneath the napkin on a slight diagonal, pressing the folds lightly in place.

# THE BUTTERFLY

A crisply starched napkin is required for this pretty fold. Lay the napkin flat. Fold two edges to meet in the center as shown. Then fold the half nearest you across the center line and over on the top of the other half, to form a long, thin rectangle.

Fold the right-hand end of the rectangle in toward the center, and with another fold double it back on itself as shown. Repeat with the left-hand side so that the double folds meet in the center.

Pull the right-hand back corner across to the left, bringing the front edge across the center line to form a triangle. Anchoring the right-hand side of the triangle with one hand, use the other hand to fold the corner back to its original position, thus creating the "wings" of the arrangement. Repeat the process on the left-hand side.

Fold the napkin twice to form a square and position it with the loose corners at the top right. Fold the top corner back diagonally to meet the lower left corner, then turn it back on itself as shown. Continue to fold the corner back and forth to create a "concertina" effect along the diagonal strip of napkin.

For best results use a crisply starched napkin to make this attractive fold. First fold the napkin lengthwise into three to form a long rectangle. Lay it horizontally with the free edge away from you. Fold the left- and right-hand ends in to meet in the center.

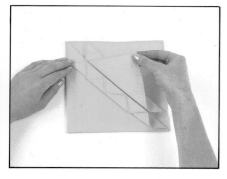

Lift the next layer of fabric from the top right-hand corner and repeat the process described above to create two parallel strips with zigzag edges.

Fold down the top right- and left-hand corners to meet in the center forming a point. Take the napkin in both hands and flip it over toward you so that the point is facing you and the flat side of the napkin is uppermost.

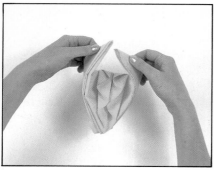

Pick the napkin up in both hands with the zigzag folds in the center. Fold it in half diagonally to form a triangle, keeping the pleats on the outside. Take the right-hand and left-hand corners of the triangle and curl them back, tucking one into the other to secure them. Stand the napkin upright on a plate as shown.

Lift the sides and pull them over toward one another to form a cone shape. Tuck the left-hand corner into the right-hand corner to secure it. Turn the napkin around and place it on a plate as shown in the main picture.

Fold the napkin in half to form a crease along the center line. Then open the napkin out again. Fold one half of the napkin lengthwise into three by bringing the top edge of the square inward to the center line and then folding it back on itself as shown. Repeat with the second half.

Fold the napkin in half lengthwise by tucking one half under the other along the center line. Lay the resulting strip flat with the three folded edges facing you. Mark the center of this strip with a finger. Fold the right-hand edge in toward the center and back on itself as shown. Repeat with the left-hand side.

Pull the top left-hand corner across toward the top right-hand corner to create a triangle. Press down gently along the folds to hold them in place. Repeat with the remaining left-hand folds, and then do the same with all the right-hand folds. Ease the folds open slightly and display the napkin with the center point facing the guest.

This miter-shaped fold can be displayed either on a flat surface (as above) or in a glass, cup, or soup bowl, which lets the flaps drape gracefully over the sides. Begin by folding the napkin diagonally to form a triangle. Then pull each corner up to the apex, as shown, to form a square.

Turn the napkin over so that the free edges lie toward you. Pull the two top flaps up and away from you. Then fold the remaining two flaps back in the same way to form a triangle.

Carefully turn the napkin over once more. Pull the two outer corners together so that they overlap. Tuck one flap into the folds of the other to hold them in place. Finally, turn the front of the "hat" to face you, and position the napkin upright. Pull the loose flaps down as shown in the main picture.

This design looks best in a conical glass but it can be adapted for a wider-based container. Although it takes a little more practice than most, it is worth the effort. First lay the napkin flat and fold it in three lengthwise. Position it as shown, with the free edge on top.

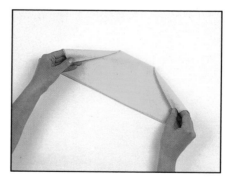

This highly effective design benefits from a well-starched napkin and is very easy to make. Begin by folding the napkin in half lengthwise. Then fold one end of the oblong backward and forward in concertina- or accordion-style folds, until just past the halfway point.

Holding the folds firmly together, fold the napkin lengthwise down the middle to bring both ends of the "concertina" together. Keeping the folds in position in one hand, fold the loose flap of the napkin over across the diagonal.

Take hold of the top left-hand and right-hand corners of the napkin with the index finger and thumb of each hand. Roll the corners diagonally toward you as shown.

Push the flap underneath the support as shown to balance the napkin. Let go of the pleats, then leave the fan to fall into position.

Without releasing your hold on the napkin, continue to roll the corners inward in one sweeping movement by swiveling both hands and napkin down, up, and over until your hands are together palms uppermost. By now the napkin should be rolled into two adjacent flutes. Release your hands and place the napkin in a tall glass, arranging it neatly.

This pretty design is ideally suited to teatime settings. Begin by folding the napkin into four – left to right, top to bottom – to form a small square. Then fold the four loose corners back across the diagonal to form a triangle.

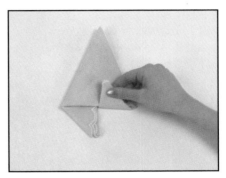

Holding the napkin firmly at the apex, fold one of the outer corners over and toward you as shown, so that it overlaps the base of the triangle. Repeat with the second corner so that the edges of both flaps meet down the center of the napkin.

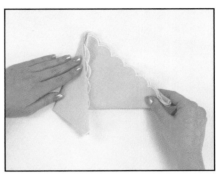

Turn the napkin over and fold the protruding flaps back over the base of the triangle. Then fold the triangle in half by pulling one of the corners over to meet the other. Finally, holding both corners firmly together, turn the napkin upright and pull the four loose corners upward as shown in the main picture.

This graceful fold is easier than it looks. Lay the napkin flat and fold it in half diagonally to form a triangle. Position it with the folded edge toward you. Bring the top corner toward you, so that the point overlaps the folded edge slightly. Carefully turn the napkin over and repeat with the other corner.

Pleat the napkin evenly across from left to right, in accordion- or concertina-style folds. Holding the straight edge of the "concertina" firmly in position, arrange the napkin in a glass. Pull the front layer of the top point toward you, creating a pointed flap over the front of the glass.

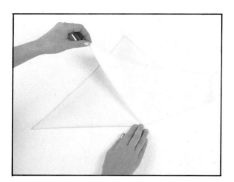

This simple fold looks elegant placed in a wineglass. Open the napkin flat. Fold it in half diagonally to form a triangle, and place the folded edge toward you. Place your index finger on the center of this edge. Using the top layer of fabric only, bring the apex down to meet the left-hand corner.

Again working with the top layer only, bring the far corner down and across to the bottom left-hand corner.

Bring the remaining top corner down and across to the lower left corner as before, forming a triangle once more. Splay the folds slightly, then turn the napkin over so that the folds are underneath. Lift the edge and roll the napkin into a loose cone shape as shown, stopping about halfway across. Fold up the bottom point and insert the napkin in the glass.

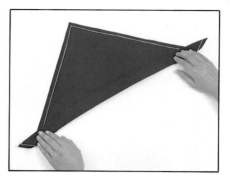

This tall candle-shade fold looks especially good if the napkin has a contrasting border. Begin by laying the napkin flat. Fold it in half diagonally to form a triangle. Turn up the folded edge about 1¼ inches (3cm), then turn the napkin over so that the fold is underneath.

Starting at the left-hand corner, roll the napkin to form a cylindrical shape.

Tuck in the end to hold the roll in place. Finally, fold down the front corner at the top as shown in the main picture.

# BUFFET ENVELOPE

This design is perfect for a smart buffet. Fold the napkin in half, and then fold it again to form a square. Take one layer of fabric from the "open" corner, and fold it diagonally over three times, with the final crease across the center. Fold the second layer of fabric in the same way, making slightly shallower folds, and tuck it under the first fold.

Fold the left- and right-hand sides to the underside, leaving a central panel in which to place the flatware. Or use the napkin as it is (without the cutlery inside) for a sit-down meal.

# POCKET NAPKIN

This simple napkin fold is embellished with a few artificial flowers tucked into the pocket. Fold the napkin in half and then in half again to form a square. Then fold it across the diagonal to form a triangle.

Position the napkin as shown with the four loose corners uppermost. Working with the top layer only, fold it down several times to make a cuff at the bottom.

Fold the next (single) corner over so that the tip touches the top edge of the cuff. Fold the next two corners over to form three tiers. Finally, turn the right and left corners of the triangle to the underside and overlap them. Position the napkin as shown in the main picture and insert the flowers.

This simple place setting is perfect for a Thanksgiving dinner. Use a sisal or straw placemat and a plain white napkin. For the decoration you will need a selection of dried flowers and grasses and three lengths of beige or wheat-colored ribbon, each about 20 inches (50cm) long.

Tie the lengths of ribbon together at one end. Braid them until the braid is long enough to tie around the napkin twice with a little left over.

Group the bunch of dried flowers and grasses together, securing them with thread or twine. Fold the napkin in half twice to form a long, thin rectangle. Lay the flowers on top of the napkin. Wind the braided ribbon around the napkin and flowers twice, then tie the ends under the napkin.

Ideal for a wedding or anniversary dinner, this lacy napkin bow is not only pretty but also easy to make. The napkins themselves should be pretty, preferably with a lace detail around the edge. For each napkin you will need about 1 yard (90cm) of wide satin ribbon and the same amount of insertion lace.

For best results, the napkin should be starched and well ironed, then folded into quarters. To cut decorative points for the ribbons and lace, fold the ends as shown and cut them diagonally.

Fold under two corners of the napkin to overlap in the center, forming the shape shown here. Iron the folds flat. Lay the ribbon and lace flat, the wrong side up, with the ribbon on top. Place the napkin on top and tie the ribbon and lace around it in a bow.

# CIRCULAR NAPKIN

This original napkin fold makes a pretty circular shape and is embellished with a bead and ribbon trimming. Paint a plain 1 inch (25mm) wooden bead with a water-based paint to match your napkin. Then paint on a pattern with a harmonizing or contrasting color. Leave the paint to dry between coats.

Fold the napkin in half once along its length. Then pleat it accordion-fashion along its length, making sure the folds are the same size.

Thread a length of thin ribbon through the bead and tie it to hold the bead in place. Wrap the ribbon around the center of the napkin, and tie it in a neat bow just below the bead. Fan the napkin out so that it forms a full circle.

# TASSEL NAPKIN RING

This tasseled napkin ring is ideal for a special occasion. You will need two tassels and approximately 16 inches (40cm) of cord per napkin, and a strong fabric glue. Attach the tassels to the cord by wrapping the loop around the cord and pulling the tassels through it.

Make the ring by feeding the cord through both loops of the tassels twice more. Make sure that the ring is large enough to slip easily over the napkin.

Using a strong glue, secure the ends of the cord to the back of the ring. Lay one end along the back and trim it. Having applied the glue to the inside of the ring as shown, wrap the remaining end over the cords, covering the trimmed end. Cut the remaining piece of cord on the inside, and clamp it in position until it is dry.

# FLORAL NAPKIN RING

This charming flower-trimmed napkin ring adds a touch of elegance to a table setting and is very easy to make. Bend a short length of florists' wire into a circle; twist the ends together to secure them.

Wind some fine fuse wire around one or two small silk flowers – chosen to coordinate with your china and table linen. Then twist the ends of the fuse wire around the circle of florists' wire to hold the flowers in place.

For covering the ring choose a fine ribbon or decorative braid. Hold one end in place with one hand. Use the other hand to twist the braid around the circle to cover it completely, beginning and ending underneath the flowers. Secure the ends with glue. Insert the napkin and add a fresh flower for the finishing touch.

# NET NAPKIN RING

For a touch of frivolity, tie your table napkins in several shades of net. For each napkin cut three different-colored rectangles of net, 18 by 13 inches (45 by 35cm). Fold each piece crosswise into three equal sections.

Fold the napkin twice to form a square, and then fold it diagonally to form a triangle. Now roll it lengthwise.

Place the lengths of net on top of each other; tie them around the napkin and fan out the ends.

This is a lovely decoration for a wedding table and makes the most of a crisp white tablecloth. Begin by taking some large white wooden rings – the kind used on curtain poles – and winding ribbon around them as shown.

Tie a bow at the top to hide the little metal ring. Then pin each ring to the front overhang of the tablecloth, spacing them evenly. Thread through a length of net, bunching it between the rings to make a good garland.

When the net is evenly arranged, attach strips of curling giftwrap ribbon to the lower edge of each ring as a finishing touch. Curl the ribbon by running the blunt edge of a pair of scissors along it.

The paper used for these crackers is similar in texture to curling giftwrap ribbon and has a lovely shiny satin finish. Cover empty bathroom tissue rolls or cardboard tubes with white sticky-backed plastic, which prevents the color from showing through. Now cut out pieces of shiny paper, twice as long as the tubes, and wide enough to go easily around them.

Wrap the tube in the paper and fix in place with double-sided tape. Don't twist the ends; scrunch them in with elastic bands, which you can then cover with strips of curling ribbon. Decorate the crackers with wrapped candies, stuck on with double-sided tape. Staple the crackers onto a strip of tinsel and trim with candies and baubles.

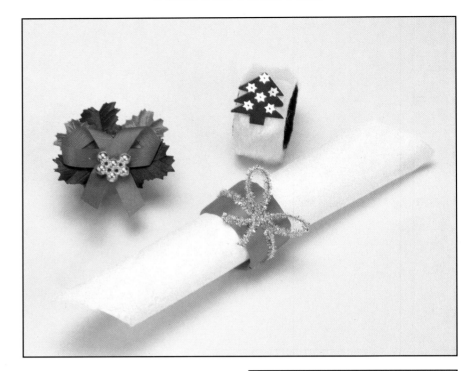

Here are a couple of ideas for jazzing up plain paper napkins. For the blue napkin, cut a star shape from a piece of cardboard – the cardboard must be slightly wider than the folded napkin. Hold the cardboard firmly in place over the napkin and spray silver or gold paint over the area. Leave the paint to dry for several minutes before you let anything else touch it.

The white napkins have a design stenciled on them with oil-based stencil crayons. You buy these separately or in packs, with ready-cut stencils. Choose your design, then place it over the area you want to stencil – in this case the corner of the napkin. Rub the crayon over a spare area of stencil. Then take the color up onto the brush and paint it over the stencil, in a circular motion.

Use the brush only over the parts you wish to show up in that color. Now switch to the next color. It is best to use a different brush for each color if you want clear color definition.

For a bit of fun at Christmastime, make some specially festive napkin rings. Each is made from a piece of cardboard tubing. The leaf sprig ring is first covered with a strip of sticky-backed plastic. Cut the plastic wide enough to go over to the inside of the ring, and cover the inside with a thinner strip of ribbon. The leaf design is a Christmas cake decoration.

Another ring has a strip of fake fur stuck to the outside, to represent snow, and green felt to disguise the cardboard on the inside. Top it with a tiny green felt Christmas tree, sparkling with sequins.

Another idea is to cover the ring with a small strip of wide satin ribbon. Glue a piece of narrower toning ribbon to the inside, folding the edges of the wide ribbon under as you go. Lastly, tie a strand of tinsel wire around the ring and finish with a bow.

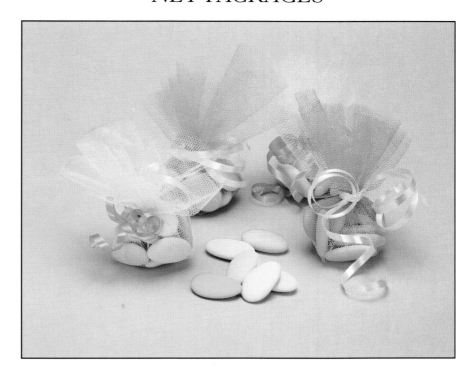

To make this simple gift for the table, fill a paper cone with chocolate buttons or candies for a children's party or with sugared almonds for adults. All you need is a small square of brightly colored wrapping paper, a ribbon rosette, and some tissue paper. Simply roll the paper into a cone from corner to corner, taping it into a nice rounded shape.

Flatten the cone slightly, positioning the top point in the center. Then fold up the bottom and stick on the ribbon rosette.

Scrunch up a little bit of tissue paper and slip it inside the cone to hold it in shape. Then fill the top with candies so that they spill out onto the point. You could attach a place card to each cone and use the cones to mark place settings at a large party.

These are cute little gifts to place beside each setting on the table. Begin by cutting out a circle of net, using a standard-size dinner plate as a guide.

Place a few pastel-colored sugared almonds into the net. Bunch it into a package with an elastic band to hold it together.

Now trim the package with curling giftwrap ribbon. (Curl the ribbon by running the blunt edge of a pair of scissors along it.) You could slip a name tag over the ribbon before tying it and use the package as an unusual place marker.

This method of decorating is known as resist painting. To create this primitive design you will need a mixture of glass and ceramic paints. Using a Chinagraph pencil, draw the design onto the plate. Remember that whatever areas you cover with the Chinagraph will appear white on the finished plate.

Carefully paint the fish using contrasting ceramic paints. These fish are colored in deep blue and yellow, but you can try other color combinations, such as purple and orange or black and gold. Now paint the border pattern in bright colors — red looks particularly attractive.

Paint the water surrounding the fish in emerald green glass paint, applying it in an undulating wave pattern to represent water currents. Use glass paint for the water as it is more translucent than ceramic paint. When the paint is completely dry, rub away the Chinagraph with a soft dry cloth to reveal the white china.

You may need to use a cloth soaked in turpentine to tidy up the edges of the pattern. Finally, protect your design with a coat of ceramic varnish.

# FASHION FLOWERS

These most unusual flowers are made from colored nylon stockings or pantyhose. First cut some pieces of copper wire 8 inches (20cm) long. Bend each into a petal shape with pliers. You need five petals for each flower. Cut the stockings or pantyhose into pieces and stretch them over the wire very tightly, binding them on with green tape.

Take five stamens (obtainable from craft stores.) Bend them in half and use pliers to attach them to the end of a long piece of copper wire, again binding them with green tape.

Now arrange the petals around the stamens. Start by placing the middle two opposite each other. Bind them, then add the other three around them. When all the petals are in place, tape around the top of the stem and continue down it to the end. When you have made several blooms, wrap them in shiny paper and tie a net bow around the outside.

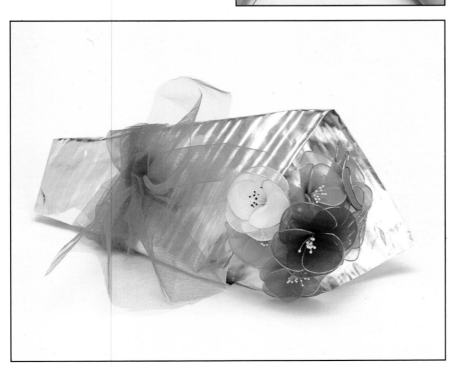

# GLAMOUR CRACKER

This beautiful cracker is not designed to be pulled but to be taken home as a memento. First take a tube of cardboard and wrap white crêpe paper around it. Insert short cardboard tubes into each end, leaving gaps of 2 inches (5cm) between the main and end sections. Cover the central and end sections on the outside with silver foil paper. Then stick pink foil paper to the inside of the end sections.

Wind a length of silver sequin waste around the center. Next take two strips of pink net and draw a piece of thread through the center of each to gather it. Tie them at each end with a strip of curling giftwrap ribbon. (Curl the ribbon by running the blunt edge of a pair of scissors along it.)

Finish by decorating the cracker with large sequins and a pink foil heart, or with some other shape if you prefer. If you like, pop a little gift inside – a handmade candy, perhaps, or even a diamond ring!

This fruit bowl is based on a wok shape, with a second bowl placed inside. Coat the inside of a wok with petroleum jelly, then apply eight layers of papier mâché all at one time. When this has dried, cut around the edge to neaten. Separate the papier mâché shape from the wok.

Repeat the process on a smaller bowl of a similar shape. When dry, mark a line partway down this papier mâché bowl, as shown. Cut, making a shallow bowl.

Apply two layers of papier mâché to the edges of both bowls. When dry, mark the wok outline on cardboard, making a register mark on the bowl and the card. Repeat with the small bowl, centering it as shown. Cut out the ring, then glue and tape the pieces together, aligning the register marks. Apply four layers of papier mâché to the rim and leave to dry.

Next, apply a layer of tissue paper. This will wrinkle, adding texture. When dry, sand and seal, then paint the bowl with water-based paint. Using blue and green children's chalks, scribble all over the surface. Brush over the surface with clear water. Repeat three more times, to create a greater depth of color. Finish with a coat of matt polyurethane varnish.

# GIFT WRAPPING

When wrapping a cylinder, avoid using very thick or textured paper as it will be difficult to fold neatly. Cut the paper longer than the cylinder (leaving extra paper at each end to cover half the cylinder's diameter), and just wider than the gift's circumference. Roll the paper around the parcel and secure with a little tape.

Wrapping square or rectangular presents isn't difficult – but perhaps your technique needs brushing up. Wrap the giftwrap tightly around the box. You can simply stick down the free edge with tape. Alternatively, for a smarter effect, fold over the top edge of the paper and stick double-sided tape underneath it, leaving a neat fold visible at the join.

Begin folding the ends of the paper in a series of small triangles as shown here. Continue around the whole circumference, making sure that the "triangles" are neatly folded into the center.

If your paper has a linear design, try to align the design so that the join is not too obvious. Fold the join section of paper down over the end of the box to make a flap; crease the fold neatly. Trim off any excess paper so there is no unnecessary bulk.

Use a single piece of tape at the center to fix all the folds in place. If the finished folds are not even, you could cheat a little by sticking a circle of matching paper giftwrap over each end of the cylinder.

Crease the side flaps firmly, and fold them over the ends of the gift. Ensure that each flap fits tightly by smoothing your hand along the side of the box and round onto the end. Fold up the remaining triangular flap, pulling it firmly along the edge of the box, and stick down. Use invisible tape (its matt surface is scarcely discernible) or double-sided for the best results.

The usual method of wrapping a sphere is to gather the paper around the gift and bunch it all together at the top. Here is a more stylish method. Put your circular gift in the center of a square of paper, making sure that the two sides of paper just meet at the top when wrapped around the gift. Cut off the corners of the square to form a circle of paper.

Bring one section of the paper to the top of the gift and begin to pleat it to fit the object as shown. The paper pleats at the top of the gift will end up at more or less the same point. Hold them in place every three or four pleats with a tiny piece of sticky tape.

Continue pleating neatly and tightly all the way round the circle. It isn't as complicated or as time-consuming as it sounds once you've got the knack! When you have finished, the pile of pleats on top of the gift should look small and neat. Then you can either cover them with a small circle of paper stuck in place or, more attractively, add a bunch of colorful ribbons.

Wrapping awkward-shaped presents is just that – awkward. The giftwrap always looks creased and untidy around the angles of the gift. The solution is not to use paper – instead, use brightly colored cellophane which doesn't crumple. Cut a square of cellophane a great deal large than your gift.

Gather the cellophane up and tie it into a bunch above the present. Fan out the excess and add some curled ribbon as a finishing touch. Alternatively, if your gift is cylindrical, roll it in cellophane somewhat longer than the parcel and gather the ends with ribbon.

S tylish, expensive-looking giftwrap can be achieved very quickly with this method of spray stenciling. Choose some plain colored paper for a base, and make your stencils from plain cardboard or paper. Cut the stencils into squares of two different sizes. Alternatively, you could use any kind of basic shape – stars, circles, or whatever.

Lay some of the shapes in a random pattern across the plain paper, holding them in place with a spot of modeling clay. Cover the whole paper with paint spray. Use car paint or craft spray paint, but only do this in a well-ventilated room.

Once the paint is dry, take off the sprayed squares and put a new random pattern of fresh squares across the paper. Overlap some of the original squares with the new ones to create interesting effects. Then spray the entire sheet with a second color of paint. Remove the squares and leave the wrapping paper to dry before using.

S tenciling is great fun to do – and so easy. Design a simple motif, then make a trace of it. With a soft pencil, scribble over the back of the trace. Next put the tracing paper face up on stencil cardboard. Draw round the design again, pressing hard so that the lines are transferred onto the cardboard beneath. Repeat the motif several times and cut out the shapes with a craft knife.

Position the cut-out stencil on plain paper, and either hold it or use masking tape to keep it in place. Mix up some poster paint, keeping the consistency quite thick. Apply the paint through the stencil, using a stiff brush. When you have finished a row of motifs, lift off the stencil carefully. Blot it on newspaper so that it is ready to use again. Leave the design to dry.

Keep repeating the process until you have covered enough paper to wrap your gift. To help you keep the spacing even between each run of motifs, add some "markers" to the stencil. Cut half a motif at the end of the run and another one above the run to mark the position of the next row. Paint the markers along with the other motifs, then use this image for re-positioning the next row.

# DESIGN WITH A SPONGE

All kinds of effects can be achieved with a sponge and some paint. You'll need a piece of natural sponge as artificial sponge doesn't produce the right effect. Choose some plain paper and mix up some poster paint to a fairly runny consistency. Test the paint on a spare piece of paper until you're happy with the color.

Dab the sponge into the paint and pat it evenly over the paper. The sponge should hold sufficient paint for about four "dabs" before you need to dip it into the paint again. You'll need to mix up a lot of paint as the sponge absorbs a considerable amount.

Rinse the sponge out well and squeeze dry. When the paper has dried, repeat the process with another color – you can use as many colors as you wish. Match the ribbon to one of the colors; see page 169 for instructions on how to create the ribbon trim shown here.

# SPATTER PATTERNS

This method makes striking wrapping paper – with apologies to artist Jackson Pollock! Creating the pattern is great fun, but rather messy. Cover your work area well with an old cloth or waste paper before you start. Begin by mixing up two or more colors in fairly runny poster pant.

Load a paintbrush with color, and, with a flicking movement, shake it across the sheet of paper. Repeat several times at various angles to cover the paper. Wait for the paint to dry.

Dip an old toothbrush in another color paint, avoiding getting the brush too full of liquid. Rub the toothbrush across the blade of a knife to cause the paint to spatter over the paper. Repeat until the spattering is as dense as you like.

Here is a novel way to disguise two lightweight gifts. Put each one in a rectangular box and wrap with giftwrap. Apply double-sided tape to the end of one box (the smallest, if they vary in size). Peel off the tape backing and press the gift against the other one making an "L" shape.

From mounting board, cut two large circles for the back wheels and two smaller ones for the front. Cut a circle for each wheel in giftwrap with ⅝ inch (1.5cm) added all around. Stick the wheel on the wrong side and snip into the edge all around. Apply double-sided tape to the circumference of the wheel and stick the snipped edge over onto the tape.

Cut giftwrap circles slightly smaller than the wheels and stick to the wrong side. Use a craft knife to cut a slice from a cardboard tube for the funnel. Apply double-sided tape in a cross shape over one end and remove the backing tape. Roll the funnel in a strip of giftwrap, then snip the excess at the top and tuck it inside.

Use a strong glue to stick the wheels to the sides of the train. Press the funnel onto the "engine." Stick three lengths of narrow giftwrapping ribbon together at one end. To coil the ribbon, pull the lengths smoothly over the blunt edge of a pair of scissors. Stick the ribbon inside the funnel for the "smoke."

156

Why not wrap one gift in another? An attractive scarf makes an ideal covering. Fold the edges of the scarf over to make a conveniently sized square and wrap the scarf around the other gift.

Tuck the top layer of each end of the scarf under the other present as shown. Then fold up the end flaps. Use a ribbon or string of beads to hold the flaps in place. Alternatively, a couple of pretty handkerchiefs make a good wrapping for a small gift such as soap. Gather the hankies around the gift and secure in a bunch with a length of lace.

It is very annoying if the giftwrap you have bought is just too small to cover your gift. The answer is to use two pieces of contrasting paper – the result can be very chic! Wrap your gift with one of the pieces of paper, using a strip of scrap paper to protect the gift from the tape. Fold in the ends neatly.

Cut the contrasting giftwrap into a strip the exact width of your package, long enough to cover the back and both ends, plus two flaps. Use this strip to hide the uncovered back of the gift and fold it over the two ends. Make two flaps on the front of the package as shown and secure with double-sided tape. Alternatively, wrap each end of the package in different paper, hiding the join with a ribbon.

Employ a humble potato to create simple yet beautiful designs. Begin by cutting a large potato in half and draw a simple design on it. Use a sharp knife or craft knife to sculpt the potato, leaving the design raised from the surface.

To ensure a regular print, draw a grid lightly in pencil on a sheet of plain paper. Then mix up fairly thick poster paint and apply it to the potato-cut with a paint brush. Print the design in the middle of each square of the grid. You should be able to do two or three prints before the color fades and needs replenishing.

Glittering giftwrap is always glamorous, and with glitter available in such a variety of colors your creativity need know no bounds! Spread out a sheet of plain colored paper. Using a bottle of glue with a fine nozzle, draw a series of simple patterns across it.

Cover the whole sheet with one design. Cut another design on another potato half. Repeat the whole process, this time printing on the cross of the grid. When the paint is thoroughly dry, erase the grid lines still visible and wrap up your gift.

Sprinkle a line of glitter across the paper. Tip up the sheet and gently shake all the glitter from one side of the paper to the other, across the glued designs, making sure that all the patterns have been well covered. Tip the excess glitter off the page onto a sheet of newspaper; the glitter can then be used again.

Now use the glue to make more designs and coat these in glitter of a different color. Localize the sprinkling of the glitter over the new patterns to be covered and leave to dry. Tip off the excess glitter and return it to its container.

Wallpaper borders can look very effective on any square- or rectangular-shaped gift. Cut a strip of border the length of one side of your wrapped gift; glue it in place along the edge.

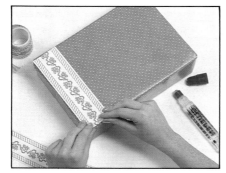

Cut another border strip for an adjacent edge. Apply glue, and position the strip so that the end of it overlaps the first strip. Now miter the overlapped corners by trimming the top strip at an angle. Do this by ruling a line between the corner of the gift and the point at which the strips overlap, as shown here.

Cut off the excess triangle of wallpaper border with a craft knife. Don't press too hard or you could damage the gift underneath. Cut two matching border strips for the other edges of the gift and repeat the mitering process with the remaining three corners.

Wallpaper is often useful as a gift covering – particularly if your gift is very large. Here a thick wallpaper with an embossed pattern has been used, giving it a touch of style and individuality. Wrap your gift, then choose some wax crayons in contrasting shades. Rub a color over the raised surface of the wallpaper to highlight one of the motifs in the design.

Choose another color, and use it to pick out another section in the pattern. (Instead of wax crayons, you could use colored pencils or chalk; the latter would need to be rubbed with a tissue afterwards to remove loose dust. The medium you choose must slide over the embossing without coloring in the whole design – paint is therefore not suitable.)

Repeat the process using a third color and continue with as many shades as you like. A tip while wrapping your gift – you'll probably find that ordinary tape will not stick to the surface of wallpaper; double-sided tape used between two folds will be more effective.

The delicate silhouette of a doily against a contrasting background color looks attractive on a gift. Wrap your gift up in plain paper and glue the doilies wherever you like. To decorate the corners of a large gift, fold a doily in half, then in half again.

Unfold the doily carefully and spread it out. Cut off one of the quarters of the doily; the folds along which you should cut will be clearly visible.

Paste the doily over one corner of the gift as shown. Repeat with alternate corners, unless your gift has enough space to take a doily over each corner without overlap. The doilies don't have to be white: silver or gold is also effective. Nor do they have to be circular – square ones would be smart on a square-sided present.

**B**rightly colored adhesive tape can give any plain wrapping paper a touch of style. A geometric design is easiest to create with tape, and the most effective; curves are rather difficult! Work out your design first and measure it out accurately on the package in pencil.

Stick the tapes in place along the pencil marks. Take care that the tapes don't stretch at all during application or they will make the paper pucker slightly. Sticky tapes are available in an enormous variety of colors, textures, and patterns; choose a strong contrast with your paper.

When re-covered in plastic, a shoe box makes a great container for a present. Put the box in the center of a piece of self-adhesive plastic and draw around it. Then draw around the shape of the sides and ends of the box so that you end up with a diagram of the "exploded" box. Leave extra plastic all round for overlaps. Cut out the pattern you have just created.

Peel the backing off the plastic and position the box carefully in the middle of the covering. Smooth the rest of the plastic up over the box, starting with the ends. Wrap the small overlap around the corners, as shown.

Smooth the plastic up over the sides, trimming off the edges to make the pieces the exact size of the sides. Fold over the overlaps around the rim. Cover the lid in the same way. For complete coordination, you could cover the inside of the box to match. Alternatively, you could line the box with coordinating tissue paper or net.

A handy gift container, ideal for homemade candies, can be made from a well-washed juice carton. Draw V-shapes on each side of the carton. These should be inverted on two opposite sides, and pointing toward the top of the carton on the other two sides. Cut cleanly along the drawn lines with a craft knife as shown.

Cover the carton with giftwrap; adhesive in spray form achieves the best results. Make sure the join lies neatly down one corner of the box. Trim the overlap at the top of the carton so that it is even. Then fold the paper over the edges, taking care that the corners are neat. Punch a hole at the apex of both the pointed sides and thread ribbon through.

This cube-shaped box is ideal for containing any kind of gift and it can be made to any size. Measure out the shape of the box onto thin cardboard, following the template on page 124. It's very important that all the squares are exactly the same size and that all the angles are right angles. Cut out the shape, and score along the fold lines – the back of a craft knife is useful for doing this.

Making a box from scratch can be a little complicated, so why not start with an empty cereal package? Take your cereal package and carefully open it out flat. Separating the joins needs care – if necessary slide a knife between the seams to part the glue, rather than tear the packet.

Bend the card carefully along the score lines, making a neat crease along each fold. Crease the flaps on the lid and base, then fold the four sides into the shape of the box.

Draw the box you want, using the template on page 252 as a reference. Make sure the lid measures the same as the width of the side panels. Cut to the new shape with a pair of scissors, and cover it with your chosen giftwrap. Spray adhesive is best, since this gives a very smooth finish, though glue in a stick form will do. When the glue has dried, cut neatly around the cardboard shape.

Stick the side flap to its opposite side as shown. You can glue this, or, alternatively, use double-sided tape. Fold in the base flap – it should fit precisely and thus give the box rigidity. Finally, close the lid flap.

Score along the new fold lines of the box using the back of a craft knife or the blunt edge of a pair of scissors. Fold the box into shape. Stick the side flap in place as shown: you can use double-sided tape or glue. Fix the two flaps on the bottom (either glue or tape them). Put in some shredded tissue as padding. Then slot in your gift and tuck the lid neatly into place.

A variation on the cube gives this box an unusual diamond shape. Draw the template on page 252 onto thin colored cardboard. Check that all the sides are the same size, and that their angles measure 90°; the angles of the lid and base should measure about 60° and 120°. Cut out the shape with a craft knife.

A cylindrical box looks much more difficult to make than it is. Wrap a piece of thin cardboard around the gift to determine the measurement of the box. Cut out the cardboard, then roll it up and stick down the edge with a length of tape. Draw and cut out a circular base, and a slightly larger circle for the lid. Attach the base with small bits of tape.

Score along the fold lines on the sides and flaps of the box with the back of a craft knife or the blunt edge of a pair of scissors. Fold the scored edges over, making sure that they are well creased for a crisp shape.

Cut a strip of cardboard slightly longer than the circumference of the cylinder. To make the lid, stick the edge of the strip to the edge of the circle with tape. Next, spread glue on some giftwrap and roll the cylinder in it. Cut the paper to fit, allowing an overlap each end. Tuck the overlap into the open end; secure. Fold the base overlap in a series of small triangles and stick to the base.

Fit the box together, sticking down the side flap with glue or double-sided tape. Fold in the base and the lid; it is the shape of these which converts the box from being an ordinary cube into the more exotic diamond shape.

Draw a circle of giftwrap slightly smaller than the base. Cut it out and glue in position, hiding all the folds, and bits of tape. Cover the lid in the same way. If you like, you can punch two holes in each side of the container and thread through short lengths of decorative braid.

# FLORAL TRIBUTE

This attractive and unusual bag will add prestige to any gift. Draw the template featured on page 252 onto a sheet of thin cardboard with the aid of a compass and a protractor; use a pencil as some of the design will need to be erased later. Cut out the circle and score along the lines of the "star" and the central octagon with a sharp edge – the back of a craft knife will do.

Take care not to overscore along the intersections of the lines, as the cardboard could eventually tear. Erase any line not scored. Bend along the edges of the octagon, being careful not to crease the sides. Then fold along the arms of the "star," to form a series of triangles (these will come together to form the container for your gift).

Folding the box needs patience, but it's not as complicated as it looks! When the folding is complete, punch holes in either side of the top of each triangle (see the template). Then thread the ribbon through the holes as shown. Arrange the curved edges so that they radiate out from the center. You can make the bag any size you want; as a guide, though, this one had a diameter of 16 inches (40cm).

# HANDLE WITH CARE

Smart handles give this box style; they are also the mechanism for closing it. Use colored cardboard for the box; if you try to cover the box pattern with giftwrap, it will lift off. Copy the template on page 253, scaling it up or down if you wish. Use a compass to draw the hands. Cut out the shape with a craft knife, taking great care with the handles and their slots.

Score along all the fold lines using the back of a craft knife; crease them well. Fold the carton into shape, and stick down the side flap with double-sided tape or glue. Fold the base down, pushing the flap inside the box to secure it.

Close the first two flaps of the lid, folding the handles up to fit. Pinch the handles together and fold the two top flaps of the lid over them, fitting the handles through the slots.

A plant is a notoriously difficult item to wrap; here's a smart solution. Measure an equilateral triangle on some colored cardboard. The length of each side should be twice the height of the plant. Use a protractor to ensure that all the angles measure 60°.

Divide each of the three sides of the triangle in half. Join all the half marks together to form an inner equilateral triangle; this will form the base. Bend the card along a ruler at each inner line as shown, then bring up the sides to form a three-dimensional triangle. Punch a hole in each apex and thread ribbon through to close the package; double-length ribbon gives a pretty finishing touch.

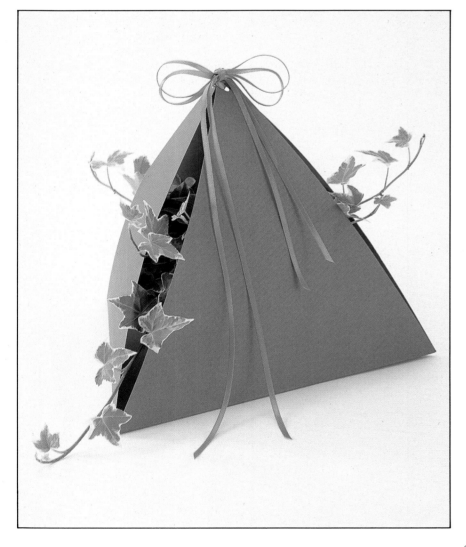

These rigid little boxes are ideal for presenting jewelry, but you can make them to fit anything you like. Choose thin cardboard, either in the color you want the finished box to be, or white so that you can cover it later with giftwrap. Measure out the template on page 253. The size of the triangular sides doesn't matter, as long as they are all the same and the base is a true square.

Cut along the exterior lines with a craft knife. If you're covering the cardboard shape with giftwrap, do it at this stage, cutting the paper to fit. Score along all the fold lines carefully, using the back of the craft knife. Then bend the box along the score marks, creasing firmly.

Punch holes in each apex and fold the box into its pyramidal shape. Thread the ribbon in and out of the four holes. Making sure that all the side-folds are tucked inside the box, tie the loose ends together with a bow.

This method is best suited to a small box as the end result is not particularly strong. From thin cardboard, cut out a cross-shaped piece as shown, made up of four sides and a base, all the same size and all absolutely square. The lid will also be a square, measuring ¼ inch (5mm) larger than the base, with sides about ¾ inch (2cm) deep.

Paste both shapes onto giftwrap. When dry cut off the giftwrap around the box and lid, leaving a small turning or flap around each edge. Fold in the flap on the left of each side of the box and glue it down as shown. Score along the edges of what will be the base, to form fold lines for the sides of the box.

Bend the sides upward. Put glue on the patterned side of the flaps of giftwrap left unfolded on each side; stick these flaps inside the box to the adjacent sides as illustrated. Crease down the sides firmly and leave to dry. Finally, fold in and glue the top lip. Treat the lid in exactly the same way.

These sachets are ideal for ties, soaps, scarves, jewelry, handkerchiefs, socks, and so forth. Onto thin cardboard, trace the template on page 253. It's probably more interesting to cover the shape with giftwrap as shown here, but you can use plain cardboard if you wish. If using giftwrap, cut out the shape and paste it onto your chosen wrapping paper.

Cut out the covered shape. Then score well along the curved lines of the ellipses which will form the overlapping ends of the package. Use the back of a craft knife or the blunt edge of a pair of scissors to make the score marks.

Stick the side flaps together with either double-sided tape or glue. Fold in the ends; if you've scored the lines sufficiently, they should pop in easily with just a little guidance. They can be reopened with no difficulty, but make sure the covering giftwrap doesn't begin to lift off the cardboard.

Gift bags are very useful as containers for awkwardly shaped presents and they can be made to any size. Find something with the required dimensions of the finished bag to serve as a mold – a pile of books should suffice. Choose a good quality, strong giftwrap for making the bag. Cut a strip of giftwrap long enough to wrap round the "mold" and fold over the top edge.

Wrap the paper around the mold; glue or use double-sided tape to join the seam at the back. Fold over the end flaps in the usual way of wrapping any package to make the base of the bag; be sure to attach sufficient tape to make the base strong.

Slip the mold out. Fold in the sides of the bag, creasing them in half at the top; fold the base up over the back of the bag. Punch two holes, spaced apart, at the top of the front and back of the bag as shown. Thread through a length of cord to form a handle; knot each end inside the bag. Repeat on the other side. Alternatively, you could thread the bag with ribbon.

This small narrow box would be ideal for giving someone a watch or a piece of jewelry – unless, of course, you make it bigger! Trace off the template on page 253 onto thin cardboard. Cut it out, and either cover it in giftwrap or, if you like the color of the cardboard, just leave it plain.

Cut around the template with small sharp scissors to trim away the excess giftwrap; take extra care with the slots and handles. Then score along all the fold lines, using the back of the craft knife or the blunt edge of the scissors.

Crease all the folds properly. Fold the box into shape and stick the side flap to the inside of the opposite side. Close the top section, being sure to fold the lid sections upright as shown, halfway across at the point where the two handles meet. Fold over the end flaps and slot them in position to close the box. Finally, close the base.

A few pretty soaps are a doubly welcome gift when wrapped in one of these pretty fabric drawstring bags. Cut a strip of cotton fabric about 2 inches (5cm) wider than you want the finished bag to be, and about 4 inches (10cm) longer. Turn in about 2 inches (5cm) at the top of each edge and run a double line of stitching along it to form a channel for the drawstrings.

A flat gift can be slipped into this pretty and useful fabric envelope. Make a paper pattern measuring about 2 inches (5cm) wider than your gift and two and a half times its depth, cutting a shallow V-shape at one end for the flap. Fold your fabric in half, then position the paper pattern with the straight edge opposite the pointed end on the fold. Pin it on and cut the fabric out.

Pin the side seams with the right sides of the fabric together, making sure the tops of both sides match. Sew the seams, leaving a gap at each end of the drawstring channel. If you don't have a sewing machine, the sewing can be done easily by hand.

With the right sides of the fabric together, pin and sew around the edges, leaving a small opening of about 3 inches (7.5cm); this is to enable the bag to be turned inside out. Turn the bag and press it. Then sew up the gap which is left. You can, of course, sew all this by hand if you prefer.

Turn the bag the right side out and press it. Get some ribbon four times longer than the width of the bag and cut it in half. Attach a safety pin to the end of one half. Thread it and the ribbon through the channels around the top of the bag so that both ends come out of one side. Knot the ends. Thread the other ribbon through both channels too, so the ends come from the other side; knot these too.

Fold the strip into an envelope shape, with the pointed flap at the top. Pin up the edges carefully and sew them in position with a double row of stitching as shown. Sew a length of ribbon onto the back of the bag with a couple of smaller stitches. Pop in the gift and tie the ribbon in a bow at the front.

A pompon bow adds a cheerful touch to a gift of any shape or size. Use the kind of ribbon which will stick to itself when moistened. Cut seven strips; four measuring about 12 inches (30cm), the other three about 8 inches (23cm). You'll also need a small piece of ribbon about 2 inches (5cm), for the central loop.

Overlap the ends of each of the long strips and moisten them. Stick them together to form a loop. Moisten the center of each loop and stick it together as shown. Cross two of the looped strips, joining them at the central point. Repeat with the other two loops. Join both crosses together so the loops are evenly spaced apart.

H ere is an easy way to achieve a very pretty effect. Choose three colors of narrow ribbon which coordinate with your giftwrap. Using one ribbon, tie it around your package in the usual way, crossing it underneath the package and knotting it tightly on top; leave long ends. Tie a length of different colored ribbon to the center point, then do the same with a third color.

Loop the three shorter lengths, and cross them over each other, fixing them together at the center. Stick the resulting star in the middle of the large rosette. Fill in the center with the tiny loop. Obviously, the length and width of ribbon can be varied, according to the size you want the finished pompon to be.

Continue tying on lengths of ribbon so that you end up with two lengths of each color (that is, four ends). Tie the central knots tightly to keep them as small as possible. Pull the ribbon length gently along the blunt edge of a pair of scissors; this will cause it to curl into ringlets. Repeat with each length until they are as curly as you want.

An alternative is to use wide gift ribbon. Tie it around the package once; make sure that the knot is as neat as possible and leave long ends. Cut two small nicks in the ribbon, dividing it evenly into three. Pull it to split the ribbon up to the knot. Run each of these lengths along the edge of a pair of scissors until they form ringlets.

The scrolled shapes of this decoration are reminiscent of the curlicues embellishing Queen Elizabeth I's signature. Wrap up your gift, and choose some giftwrapping ribbon to match or contrast with the colors of the giftwrap. Hold the end of the ribbon in one hand and form a loop as shown, leaving a small tail.

Make a corresponding loop below, forming a figure-of-eight shape. This will be the size of the finished bow; adjust the proportion of the loops at this stage if you want a bigger or smaller bow. Continue folding loops of the same size until you have as many as you want – seven at each end is usually enough.

Check that all the loops are the same size, and pinch them all together by wrapping a piece of sticky tape around the middle. You can then hide this by wrapping a small piece of matching ribbon over it. Attach it to the gift with double-sided tape.

This bow, with its floppy loops, gives a soft, casual effect. You'll need about 6 feet (2m) of acetate or craft ribbon, 1 inch (2.5cm) wide. Cut off about 12 inches (30cm) of ribbon; wind the rest round your fingers. Holding the ribbon firmly, make a notch in both edges with a pair of scissors as shown, cutting through all the layers of ribbon.

Take the ribbon off your fingers and notch the edges of the opposite side of the loops. Flatten the loops so that the notches match in the center and loops are formed on either side. Take the 12 inches (30cm) length of ribbon and tie it tightly around the notches as shown.

Starting with the innermost loop on one side of the folded bow, gently pull each loop away from the other loops and into the center of the bow. You'll end up with each loop being visible, thus forming the shape of the finished rosette.

# TWISTED TRIM

This trimming can be made to match or contrast with the wrapping. You will need the type of ribbon which sticks to itself when dampened. The smallest strip of ribbon measures about 8 inches (20cm); cut it out and twist it into the shape of a figure "8."

Twist the ribbon shape to form a point at each end, as shown. Secure it in position by dampening the tape. Cut the next strip, about 3 inches (7.5cm) bigger; repeat the process. Put the small shape on top and in the center of the new shape; fix it in place.

Make four other figures-of-eight, cutting each one about 3 inches (7.5cm) longer than the last. Pile them all up and fix them together in the center. Put the decoration on your gift and attach it by wrapping ribbon around it and the package. Finally, arrange it so that each loop is raised above the others and not overlapping as they're inclined to do!

# A POINT TO REMEMBER

You couldn't distinguish this pointed pompon from a store-bought version – yet it's a fraction of the price! Use ribbon which sticks to itself when moistened. Make a small loop by wrapping the ribbon around your thumb. Moisten the ribbon and fix it in place. Now twist the ribbon back on itself to form a pointed loop, as shown; stick it in position.

Go on looping the ribbon in twists, spacing them evenly as you go. It is fairly fiddly, but keep trying – you'll soon master the technique. You'll probably need to wait a minute between each fixing for the ribbon's glue to dry before turning the next loop.

Continue winding outward in a circle until the bow is as big as you want; cut off the ribbon, leaving a small tail just visible. Attach the pompon to the gift with double-sided tape.

It's hard to believe that these pretty flowers and the butterfly are made from pantyhose and fuse wire. Cut up a pair of discarded pantyhouse. Cut some fuse wire into lengths, some shorter than others, suitable for making petals. Make a circular shape out of each length and twist the ends together.

Put a piece of the pantyhose fabric over a wire circle and pull it tight, making sure that the whole circle is covered. Fix it in position by firmly winding matching cotton around the twisted stem of the wire. Cut off the excess fabric.

Take seven petals. Put the smaller ones in the center, and bind them all tightly with thread. Bend the petals around until you're happy with the look of the flower. Tie up your package with ribbon and attach the flower with double-sided tape. The butterfly is made in just the same way: the two pairs of "petals" are bound together with thread, then bent into the shape of wings.

How to give a tall thin present even more presence! Take a spool of gift ribbon – the sort that sticks to itself when moistened. Roll a length around your thumb to form a small circle. Moisten it and stick in position.

Make another ring, larger than the first; stick that down, too. Make another circle, and another, ensuring that their increase in size is in the same proportion each time. Four circles is about the maximum the ribbon can take before flopping slightly and thus losing the crispness of the decoration.

This decoration looks best on a rectangular gift. Lay 26 inches (66cm) of woven ribbon flat. Measure 5 inches (13cm) from one end of the ribbon and mark both edges. Then mark along the ribbon's length a farther 4 inches (10cm), 3 inches (7.5cm), 2 inches (5cm), 3 inches (7.5cm), 4 inches (10cm). Using one piece of thread, pick up tiny stitches at each mark along one edge.

Run a similar gathering thread up the other edge of ribbon, making sure that the stitches are exactly level on both sides. Gather up the loops as shown; it's easiest to knot the two threads together at one end of the gathers and ease the loops along.

Pull the thread tight to make properly formed loops; sew the joins in place and cut off the excess thread. Tie the ribbon around the gift and use double-sided tape to attach the loops in the center of the long side of the gift. Snip a diagonal cut at the ends of the ribbon tails.

It is quite easy to paint wide ribbon to coordinate with your giftwrap. And the results are stunning! Choose a giftwrap with a simple design. Decide whether you want the ribbon to be a positive version of the paper's design, like the blue example shown here, or a negative one, like the black and white suggestions. Experiment with poster paint on your chosen ribbon.

Keep the design very simple and stylized. When you're happy with your pattern, paint enough ribbon to wrap up the gift, leaving sufficient for a fairly large bow. Let the ribbon dry thoroughly before tying it around the package. If the paint does crack a little when tying up the ribbon, simply touch it up and leave it to dry again.

Crêpe paper is the ideal material to make a stylish ruffle. There's such a range of colors to choose from, too. For each ruffle, cut two strips of crêpe paper, one a little wider than the other. They should both be half as long again as the circumference of the package.

Lay the two strips flat, with the narrower one on top. Sew them both together with matching thread, running a gathering thread down the center. Gather the strips slightly.

Gently stretch the crêpe paper between both hands along the entire length of the strip; this will create a more ruffled effect. Do each strip separately, then make another ruffle. Wrap the ruffles around the gift, sticking the ends with tape. Tie narrow cord in the middle of the strips to hide the gathering stitches. Fluff up the crêpe ruffles on either side.

This elegant two-tone cord with its matching rosette is made of twisted rickrack. Choose two colors of rickrack braid to coordinate with your giftwrap. Buy about 3 feet (1m) of both colors. Wrap one piece of braid around the zigzags of the other, twisting them so that they fit snugly together. Do enough to wrap around your gift and press the braid with a cool iron.

Twist some more braid together to make the rosette – the length you need depends on the size of the rosette. Take a needle and thread through each point of one side of the twisted rickrack.

Having threaded about 18 inches (45cm), gently pull the thread, easing it along the rickrack. This will cause the rickrack to coil up on itself; arrange it into a flat circle, sewing it together as you go. When you have a large enough rosette, cut the braid and sew the edges neatly under. Tie the long length of braid around the package and sew in position; sew on the rosette.

A small posy of pretty rosebuds is always acceptable – make as many as you like! Cut a small length of ribbon – about 2–3½ inches (6–9cm), depending on the width of ribbon you've chosen. Fold the ribbon in half, with the right sides together, and join the two ends with a small seam. Run a gathering thread around one edge.

Pull the gathering thread tight to form the rosebud; sew it firmly across the base. Make another two or three buds and sew them all together at the base; you may need to add the occasional supporting stitch at the top edges to hold the buds close together.

The leaves add an attractive contrast. They are made from a strip of green ribbon, two corners from which have been folded over to form a point. Fix with double-sided tape since glue can leave a mark on ribbon. The illustration below shows the rosebuds grouped on a length of ribbon twice the width of the flowers, set off with narrow green ribbon.

A winning idea for any gift! Cut a length of fairly wide ribbon; you'll need about 12 inches (30cm) for each rosette. Fold it in half with the right sides of the ribbon together; sew up the two ends to form a seam.

Using tiny stitches, gather up one edge of the ribbon. Pull the gathering thread tight, arranging the rosette into a neat circle. Finish it off by sewing across the base. Make as many rosettes as you need and attach them to your package with double-sided tape.

What do you do when you haven't any giftwrap and the stores are shut? You use newspaper! The flower on top gives the package a stunning and stylish finish. To create the flower, cut several lengths of newspaper, some about 6 inches (15cm) wide, some a little narrower. Fold one strip in half lengthwise, and make a series of cuts along its folded edge, as shown here.

You can make these decorations in a single color, but they look more effective if you choose several. For each twist, you need three squares of tissue for the outer color, two for the middle color, and two for the inner (most visible) section. The squares needed for the inner section are smaller than those for the outside; the middle leaves must be of a size in between.

When you've cut along the whole length, roll up the resulting looped fringe. Secure it at the base by winding a piece of sticky tape round it. Fluff out the "petals" of the flower.

Pick up the squares in order, putting one on top of the other: outer color first, then the middle, then the inner squares. Position them so that the corners of each square are at a different angle, as shown. Put a couple of stitches through the center point to secure all the squares together. Leave some thread hanging.

Use up all the strips of paper in the same way. Gather the sections together, smaller ones on the outside. Join them all with tape; leave the ends unstuck and use them to attach the flower to the gift. You can even match the paper to the recipient: for example, a financial newspaper for a businessman, a comic for a child.

Fold the whole thing in half and half again, twisting the folded point at the base to form the shape of the "flower." Pull the thread out at the point, and wind it tightly around the twisted base to secure it. "Fluff" out the finished decoration. Make several "flowers" and group them together on your gift.

Frothy net is a very attractive decorative feature, and silver glitter adds a sparkle and a touch of glamour. Cut a strip of net long enough to wrap twice around the perimeter of the gift; make its width about 6 inches (15cm) wider than the length of the package.

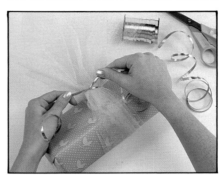

Gather the net in small pleats and wrap it around the middle of the package, as shown. Tie the net with narrow gift ribbon and leave the ends of the ribbon trailing. Gently pull apart the net tails. Cut another piece of net the same width as the first piece and twice the depth of the existing "frill." Thread it underneath the frill and secure it with ribbon as before.

Put some silver glitter in a bowl and dab glue along the raw edges of the net. Dip the net into the glitter (this involves holding the package upside down). Shake off the excess glitter and leave the glue to dry. Curl up the trailing lengths of ribbon by pulling them against a blunt scissor blade.

An interesting effect is achieved by attaching three-dimensional decorations all over your package. Wrap your gift in plain colored paper. For the butterflies, take a strip of contrasting plain paper and fold it in half. Draw a butterfly shape on thin cardboard. Cut it out and trace round half of it, as shown, onto the colored paper. Draw as many shapes as you want to cover the gift.

Cut out the butterfly shapes and fold them on both sides of the halfway fold, to give them bodies. Use glue or thin strips of double-sided tape to attach them in a random pattern to the parcel. Alternatively, tie lots of little bows of the same size using contrasting ribbon; scatter them over your gift using double-sided tape.

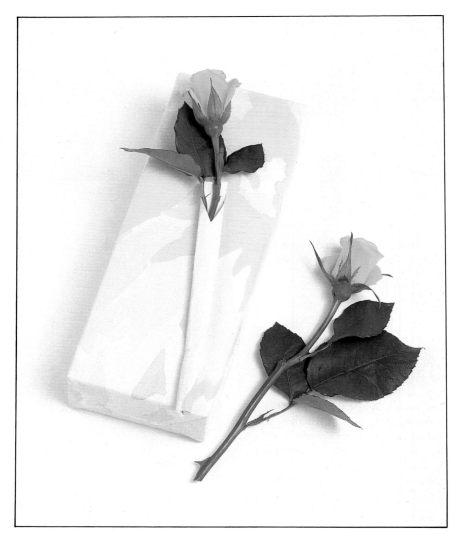

A pretty arrangement of dried flowers is a lovely idea for somebody with a fall or winter birthday. You can pick grasses and seedheads in the country or you can dry flowers from your own garden; it's fun and quite easy. Alternatively, you can buy them, though of course it's more expensive that way. Cut the dried plants all the same length.

Bunch the flowers together; when you're happy with them, wrap sticky tape around the stalks. Hide the tape by winding ribbon over it. Tie ribbon round the package, finishing off with a knot. Attach the little bouquet by tying its trailing ribbons over the knot, and trim off the ends of the bouquet ribbon. Using the ends of the other ribbon, finish off by making a pretty bow over the bouquet.

What a lovely bonus to receive with a gift – a beautiful fresh flower. This works most effectively with a long, thin gift, showing off a single bloom to perfection. First choose your flower. Trim off any excess leaves and, in the case of roses, thorns. You should end up with just one sprig of leaves.

To prevent the flower from staining the giftwrap or making it damp, cover the end of the stalk with plastic wrap. Then cut a narrow strip of matching giftwrap; wrap it around the length of the stalk, fixing it at the back with tape. Cut a small "V" shape at the top of the paper tube, and attach the bloom to the package with double-sided tape.

Craft foil is the perfect material for creating this decoration. Use a compass to draw four circles; the ones shown here measure 3 inches (8cm), 2½ inches (6.5cm) 2 inches (5cm), and 1½ inches (4cm) in diameter. Draw an inner ring of ¾ inch (2cm) in the center of each circle. Rule lines to divide the circles evenly into eighths. Cut along the lines to the inner circle to make eight segments.

Roll each segment of the circle into a cone; use a dab of glue to secure it. Make sure that each cone shape has a good sharp point by rolling it fairly tightly. The process is a bit fiddly; you may find it easier to roll each cone around the point of a stencil to give it shape. Repeat with the other circles.

Starting with the largest star shape, glue all the stars inside each other, positioning the points of each star between those of the preceding ones. When the glue is dry, gently bend each cone of the middle two stars toward the center, to fill in the central space, so forming a semi-circular, three-dimensional star.

Brightly colored drinking straws lend themselves to decorating gifts. Look for colors to coordinate with your giftwrap. The straws can be made of paper or plastic; both work well. Select the colors you want and cut four straws in half; discard one of each half. Cut another four straws in two, leaving one section slightly longer than the other; retain both pieces.

Place four halves, one of each color, together over a central point, in a star shape. Staple them together. Do the same with the other slightly longer straws and their shorter counterparts so that you end up with three stars of slightly different sizes. With the smallest on top and largest on the bottom, staple all three together. Attach the triple star to the package with double-sided tape.

These flowers will pretty up any package at very little cost – they're made from tissues. Open out a tissue, and fold it in half lengthwise. Trim away half of the top layer (that is, a quarter of the tissue) along the whole length as shown – this prevents the "stalk" of the finished flower from being too bulky.

Paper fans are simple to make but can look stunning, used either singly or in a row to create a ruffle around your gift. Cut a strip of paper the width you'd like the fan to be when opened, and three times the length. Fold it in half widthwise, then fold it up in small, even pleats, starting with the folded end. Create a sharp crease along the pleats by running them firmly between your fingers.

Tuck in the top corner of one end very slightly and gather up the tissue in very small pleats, gradually turning the "flower" round as you go. When the gathering is completed, fold in the top corner of the end of the tissue as before.

When you have pleated the entire length, hold the pleats together with the folded edge of the strip on top. Bend the fan in half and stick the two folded edges together with sticky tape along their length as shown. Make sure that the tape continues right to the outer edge so that the join cannot be seen when the fan is open.

Give the "stalk" a couple of twists to make it firm. Bind it tightly with thread and tie it securely. Make as many flowers as you need for your gift – you can make an entire bouquet if you like and wrap it up in a paper doily. Tie the flowers together with a ribbon and make a bow. Then attach the bouquet to your gift.

Open out the fan and apply double-sided tape to its flat side; stick the fan in position on your gift. Care is needed in deciding how big to make the fan – too big and the present will be swamped, too small and it will look insignificant. It might be worthwhile experimenting with rough fans cut from newspaper first, to get the scale right before cutting your giftwrap.

A sweet treat for kids of all ages! Fruit jellies with plain cellophane wrappers look best because of their clear colors, but you can use alternatives such as fudge or peppermints. Select five or six of the chosen candies, and hold them in a bunch by one end of their wrappers.

An added bonus on this gift is the sweet-smelling pouch of potpourri. Select some fabric which will tone with your giftwrap. The fabric should be fine, but not loosely woven; the scent of the potpourri can then easily diffuse through the material, but the petals and dust cannot. Cut out a piece of fabric measuring about 6–8 inches (15–20cm) square.

Take a narrow piece of ribbon and tie all the candies together tightly. If the wrapper ends are a little short, it may help to bind them first with sewing thread. Leave a reasonably long piece of ribbon on each side of the bunch of candies so that you can attach it easily to the package.

Put enough potpourri in the center of the fabric to make a generous sachet – a good handful should be just right. If you can, choose a perfume which will match your present – rose potpourri would be ideal for a rose bowl, lavender for lavender-scented soaps. You could even use dried herbs to create a bouquet garni for a cookery book!

Tie the same ribbon around the package, leaving the ends long. Then tie the candies to the center point as shown. Curl up each ribbon end by pulling it gently along the blunt edge of a pair of scissors. Try to coordinate your giftwrap with the chosen confectionery – black and white paper with licorice, for example, would look very attractive.

Pick up the four corners of the fabric to form a bundle. Wind sewing thread tightly around the neck of the bundle, and knot the thread securely. Tie the potpourri bunch very firmly in case the recipient uses the bag later in her closet. Hide the thread by tying a piece of ribbon around it to match the ribbon on the package. Tie the potpourri to the gift using a little more matching ribbon.

# TASSEL ATTACHMENTS

Silky tassels give a luxurious look to a gift, especially if they are made of sparkling Lurex yarn. Cut a piece of thin cardboard the length you'd like the tassels to be. Wind yarn around the cardboard until it is the density you want for the finished tassel.

Thread a length of yarn through all the strands. Tie it firmly at the top of the cardboard as shown, leaving the ends long. Cut through the strands of yarn at the opposite end of the cardboard.

Tie some yarn around the tassel, about ½ inch (1cm) from the top. Trim the ends to the length of the tassel fringe. Make another tassel. Twist together four long lengths of yarn and tie them round the package in the usual way. Then tie the tassels at each end. Regular yarn or thick rug yarn woud look just as effective.

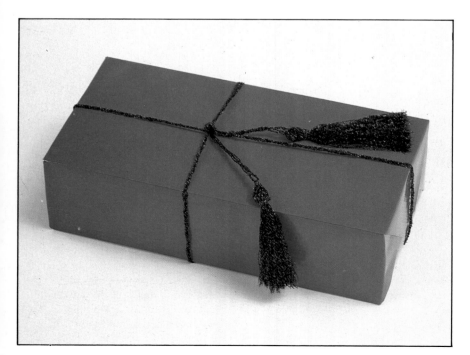

# SEQUIN SHEEN

The metallic sheen of sequins, and the strip of metallic plastic from which they are pressed, looks rather chic. Sequin waste – that is, the strip of metallic plastic – can be bought by the yeard or meter from good craft stores. This idea looks best on rectangular flat packages. Wrap a piece of sequin waste around the length of the gift; fix it with tape.

Take another strip of sequin waste and join the two ends to make a large loop. Use sticky tape to fix them, making sure the holes overlap so that the join is almost invisible.

Put a strip of threaded sequin trim of the same color across the middle of the loop. Remove a few loose sequins so that you can tie the trim in position. Repeat with another length of trim; space the two evenly apart in the center of the loop to form a bow. Attach the bow to the package with double-sided tape. Sequin trim as a gift tie in its own right gives a glamorous finish to any gift.

Pick out the colors of your giftwrap to make your own pretty plaits. From narrow fabric ribbon – ½ inch (2mm) wide – choose either three colors which feature in your giftwrap or, if you prefer, three lengths of the same shade. Knot them together at one end, leaving small tails.

Start braiding the ribbon. This is easier if you weigh down the knot with something; the scissors will do fine. Keep braiding as evenly as possible, moving the weight along the growing length of braid as necessary.

When you've finished, tie the braid round your gift in the usual way. Before knotting it, undo the knot you made when you began braiding; tie a single tight knot to keep both ends of the braid in place. Loop each tail back on itself, dabbing on a tiny spot of glue and fixing it in the center beside the knot.

For an elaborate and slightly saucy effect for your gift, select some slotted lace and some ribbon to coordinate with your giftwrap. Measure the amount of ribbon needed to tie up the package; you will need twice as much lace. Thread the ribbon through the slots.

Gather the lace up on the ribbon. Wrap it around the length of the package and sew it together at the back. Then wrap the width; sew that, too. Finish by tying an extra bow at the intersection of the two laces. Any gift looks pretty simply tied with lace, even if the lace can prove a little expensive. Look out for remnants on notion counters or market booths.

Windmills are cheerful and fun for people of all ages – not just children! Cut out a square of plain colored paper which complements your giftwrap. Measure a square of about 9 inches (23cm), depending on the size of windmill you want; make sure the corners are right angles. Cut out the square and draw straight lines between the opposite corners.

Cut along these lines, starting from the corners and leaving about 1 inch (2.5cm) uncut in the center. Bend up one side of each cut corner to the center, as shown, anchoring it with double-sided tape.

To attach the windmill to a "pole," take a colored plastic drinking straw and insert a two-pronged paper fastener in the end. Open the prongs out a little so the fastener stays firm. Pierce the center of the windmill with another paper fastener. Pass its prongs through the one inserted in the straw, then open them out. Attach the straw and windmill to the parcel with double-sided tape.

A smartly dressed gift for a smartly dressed man – or woman! This is suitable for a tall thin gift. Wrap it up in paper of a color and design that is plausible for a shirt. Cut out a "collar" shape as shown from stiff white paper. Fix it in position around the top of the package with glue or double-sided tape.

Using patterned ribbon for the tie (such as this elegant Paisley design), wrap it around the collar and knot it like a tie. Before pulling it tight, put some glue or double-sided tape on the collar where the tie should sit. Position the tie correctly and tighten the knot. Finally, fold over the two corners of the collar shape to make an elegantly formal shirt.

Victorian ladies created beautiful pictures using pressed flowers. Why not make a miniature version for a pretty gift tag? Pick up a selection of flowers and leaves and lay them face down on blotting paper. Press another layer of blotting paper on top, keeping the flowers as flat as possible. Place the flowers between the pages of a heavy book and leave them for at least a week.

Take out the flowers. Make a template for a perfect oval by folding a small sheet of paper in half and half again. Draw a curve across the corner as shown and cut it out. Trace round the unfolded shape on white cardboard. Make a slightly larger oval from colored cardboard to match the giftwrap.

Giftwrap can prove so expensive these days, so why not make your own gift boxes? Here, some plain cardboard boxes have been covered in hand-marbled paper. Fill a large bowl with water. Then mix some solvent-based paint such as ceramic paint, or some artists' oil colors, with a little mineral spirit. Use a paint brush to drop successive colors onto the surface of the water.

Stick the two ovals together, so that the larger one forms a frame for the tag. Arrange the pressed flowers on the white oval to your satisfaction. Glue the flowers in position, using a tube with a very fine nozzle. Leave the arrangement to dry thoroughly. Punch a hole in the top of the tag. Write the message on the back and tie it to the gift.

Stir the mixture with the handle of your paint brush or an old stick until you have a pleasant swirling pattern. An alternative way to form a pattern is to blow the paint across the surface of the water.

Wearing rubber gloves to protect your hands, put the paper onto the surface of the water, then lift it off immediately. The swirls of paint on the paper will create a marbled effect. When the paper is dry, neatly cover a small box, carefully folding the paper around the corners and sticking it down with glue or double-sided tape.

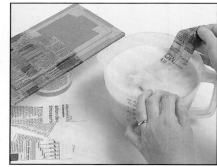

Use 2 by 4 inches (5 by 10cm) pieces of paper to papier mâché both the box and lid, applying three layers. Dry the pieces on a wire cooling rack in a warm place. Lightly sand them and then apply two coats of white water-based paint.

This durable, papier mâché chocolate box would make a lovely gift. Using a ruler and set square, mark and cut the following pieces from cardboard: four 10¾ by 6 inches (27 by 15cm), and two each measuring 9¼ by 4½ inches (23.5 by 11.5cm), 2 by 10 inches (5 by 25cm), and 2 by 5 inches (5 by 12.5cm). Glue and tape the largest pieces into two pairs and the narrow strips into a rectangle.

Paint the insides of the box and lid with blue gouache, made up to the consistency of heavy cream. Draw the outer lines in pencil first, then go over them with a waterproof black felt-tip pen. Do not worry about slight irregularities – they add to the effect. Apply one coat of polyurethane varnish.

Glue the walls of the box to the base. Hold them with masking tape until the glue has set. Then remove the masking tape and reinforce all joins with brown tape. Join the remaining two pieces with glue and tape, then center them on the lid. Use the blunt end of a pair of kitchen scissors to ease the brown tape into the joins.

Apply three more coats, this time of gloss acrylic varnish (painted directly over gouache, it would make the colors run). When this has dried, the ribbon can be fixed in place with epoxy resin glue. Cover the join with heart shapes cut from adhesive-backed silver paper strip.

Stencil your own wooden presentation boxes to add a little extra to a small gift. Choose single motifs and use either quick-drying stencil paints or stencil crayons. Mask off a small motif from a large stencil, then tape the acetate in position to complement the box shape. Stencil the box top and sides, mixing designs to create an attractive arrangement.

Making your own giftwrap is great fun for a beginner at stenciling. Choose small, all-over motifs (see pages 37 and 247) and stencil with one or two different colored stencil crayons. Use plain art paper and work across it, lining up the motifs as shown. Rub the crayon on the corner of the acetate and then collect the color onto a stencil brush for stencilling.

Make a colored border on the lid by cutting a piece of cardboard slightly smaller than the box top. Position it centrally and stencil around the edge. Finish off the box by gluing on lengths of satin ribbon, bows, or self-adhesive giftwrap ribbon. You could also line the box with colored tissue paper.

Gold spray on dark paper makes a rich, dramatic giftwrap ideal for a man's Christmas gift. Use the same stencil design, but tape liner paper around the edge to act as a mask. Spray lightly through each motif. Wait a few moments for it to dry, then move onto the next area. Matching gift tags can easily be made by cutting out one motif and gluing it onto folded cardboard.

A three-dimensional Santa Claus tag, complete with fluffy beard, provides a jolly festive decoration on a gift. Draw a fairly large rectangle on thin red cardboard; make sure that all the corners are right angles. Score down the middle and fold the cardboard, creasing it well. Draw an inverted "V" for Santa's hat, and a curve for his chin; cut them out with a craft knife.

Curve the hat and chin outward to give them a three-dimensional look, then draw in the eyes and mouth. Form a beard from a small piece of cotton swab, and stick it in position with a dab of glue. Do the same with the fur trim on the edge of the hat and the pompon on its tip. Punch a hole in the back of the label, then write your message and tie the tag on the package.

A heavenly messenger bears the greetings on this Christmas gift. Cut a quarter section of a circle from light cardboard to form a narrow cone for the body. On a folded piece of paper draw one arm and one wing against the edge of the fold as shown, so that when they are cut out, you will have a pair of each.

Make the cone and cover it with silver paper (aluminum foil would do). Trace the arm and wings onto silver paper. Cut them out and glue them in their relevant positions on the body.

Make the head by rolling up some white tissue paper into a firm ball, twisting the ends of the tissue tightly to form a "neck." Glue the head into the top of the cone. Tie a scrap of tinsel into a loose knot and stick it on the head as a halo. Make a scroll from white paper. Write on your message and stick it between the angel's hands. Attach the angel to the gift with double-sided tape.

188

## SEASON'S GREETINGS

Draw any festive shape you like onto thin cardboard; this one is a Christmas stocking. Cut out the shape and cover it with bright paper; try to coordinate the colors with those in the giftwrap you use for your present.

If your giftwrap has a particular theme in its design, make a tag to echo it. To ensure that your design is symmetrical, fold a piece of paper in half and draw on half the design against the outline through both layers of paper. Open out and use this as a template for the design. Cover a piece of light cardboard with giftwrap and trace around the template.

Cut around the outline and punch a hole at the top of the tag. Write your message and tie the tag onto the parcel. You could cheat a little when designing the shape of your tag by tracing an illustration from a magazine or by using the outline of a cookie cutter.

## EASTER MESSAGE

This cute rabbit tag tells the kids who gave them their Easter present. Draw the shape of a rabbit onto white cardboard; if you're not good at drawing, you could cheat by tracing the outline of a rabbit from a magazine or book illustration. When you're happy with your design, cut it out.

Either paint the bunny shape, or cover it with brown paper (or whatever color suits your giftwrap; a red or even green rabbit would be fun). Next, take a piece of cotton swab and roll it into a ball for the tail. Stick it in position with a dab of glue. Make a hole in the rabbit's head for some ribbon. Write your message and tie the tag to the gift.

## PATTERN MATCH

Give your presents a co-ordinated appearance by creating matching tags. For simple fold-over tags you need to select a giftwrap that has a small design. Take a piece of giftwrap and rule a rectangle on it, twice the width of the required tag. (Outline a section of the design where the motif is visible when isolate.) Ensure the corners are perfect right angles, then cut the tag out.

Paste the tag onto thin cardboard; choose a color which picks up a shade in the gift wrap. When the glue is dry, cut around the piece of gift wrap. Fold the card in half and punch a hole in the corner. Thread a ribbon through the hole and tie it onto the gift. Alternatively, you can cut out a single image. Stick it onto cardboard and cut around the outline, as with the panda tag.

## FUN FOLD-OUT

If you have a long message for the recipient of your gift, this fold-out tag leaves lots of room. Select a giftwrap design that has a fairly large repeat. One motif must have sufficient space around it so that it can be cut out without including any others. Draw a rectangle around the motif, ensuring that all the corners are right angles.

Cut the rectangle out with a craft knife. Next, cut out a piece of thin cardboard the same height as the chosen motif and exactly three times its width. Fold the cardboard in three widthwise, creasing the folds well. Then fold the top two sections back on themselves, as shown. Mark the folds in pencil first to be sure they are straight.

Cut the motif from the giftwrap precisely in half. Glue each half onto the top two sections of the folded card. They should fit exactly, but if necessary trim the top and bottom to form a straight edge. Try matching the colors of the lining cardboard with the giftwrap; in the example shown here, red or even black cardboard could have been used instead of white, for a different effect.

190

A different way of matching the label to the paper is to create a larger version of a shape which appears in the giftwrap. Begin by drawing a scaled-up shape of the motif from the paper. Use it as a template from which to trace the design onto the colored cardboard.

For this idea to be really effective, the color of the tag should be as close as possible to that in the giftwrap. A layer of tissue laid over the cardboard of a near-match, as shown, might make all the difference to duplicating the final color. Cut out the shape, and punch a hole to enable you to tie it to the gift.

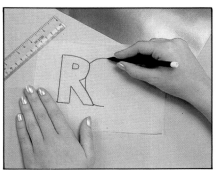

There can be no doubt who these presents are for! It's fun to make a tag out of the initial or – even better – the full name of the recipient. First draw the shape of the letters you want onto a piece of tracing paper. Make sure that the letters in a name interlock sufficiently.

When you're happy with the result, trace the letters (or single initial) onto colored cardboard, pressing hard to make a clear outline. Use a ruler where there are straight sections to a letter.

Next, cut out the shape using a craft knife, carefully following the traced lines. Punch a hole in a position where the weight of the tag will make it hang well on the gift.

Incorporate a motif from the design of your giftwrap to make a fun three-page tag. It will work with any design involving a trailing string – balloons, kites, balls of yarn, and so on. The motif is stuck on the sloping top edge of the middle "page" of the card. Cut out the motif from giftwrap. Then experiment with a sheet of white paper to get the best shape for your card.

The slanting angle of the top edge is achieved by cutting a truncated triangular shape. Having worked out the shape you want, trace around your experimental tag onto thin colored cardboard. Don't forget to leave a bit of card protruding from the top slanting edge in the shape of the motif, as shown. Cut out the tag.

Score the two fold lines of the tag using the back of a craft knife and crease them firmly. Glue the motif in position on the middle page and draw a long string trailing down. Close the card and draw another string on the front, making sure it is continuous with the string on page two. Write the recipient's name as if it were part of that string.

Create a stylish effect by matching the tag to the ribbon. Plain ribbon with a strongly patterned paper is attractive, but a plaid ribbon with plain paper can look stunning. And if you don't have any ribbon, even a strip of fabric cut out with pinking shears will suffice! Glue a length of ribbon or fabric onto thin cardboard to make it rigid.

Trim away any excess cardboard. Fold the stiffened ribbon over and cut it to the length you want the finished tag to be. Punch a hole through your newly created tag and thread a piece of contrasting narrow ribbon through the hole to tie it to the package. Trim the edges of the tag to match the ends of the bow.

Used greeting cards can often be turned into very acceptable gift tags. Sometimes, as here, the design lends itself to forming a tag. Cut very carefully around the lines of the motif you want to use. Make a hole with a punch and thread a ribbon through the hole – no one would guess the tag had a previous life.

There is such a variety of stickers on the market that you're sure to find one which will make an ideal label. Take a piece of thin colored cardboard; this will form the background for the sticker. Draw a rectangle onto the cardboard, twice the width you wish the finished tag to be.

Cut out the rectangle with a craft knife and score down the center to form the fold; crease well. Remove the sticker from its backing and place it in position on the front of the tag. Punch a hole in the back "page" of the tag, near the fold. Write your message inside and hang the tag on the gift.

Sometimes a little imagination is needed to give the tag a new and store-bought look. Here, the shape of the tag is outlined on the cardboard in red with a felt-tip pen. Draw the outline lightly in pencil first to be absolutely sure it is the right size and shape to create the finished label.

What fun for a child to see Frosty and know that the snowman's hiding a gift! Wrap up a cylindrical gift in paper to form the body of the snowman. Crush newspaper into a shape for the head and stick it on top of the gift. Cover the body with cotton swabs, sticking them on with dabs of glue. Create a face from bits of paper and stick it in place.

For the hat, you need a strip of cardboard, plus a circle big enough to make the brim. Draw an inner circle in the brim, the diameter of Frosty's head. Cut it out to form the "lid" of the hat. Roll the strip of cardboard up to form the crown of the hat; stick it in place with tape.

Stick on the top of the hat. Then attach the brim, putting strips of tape inside the crown. Paint the hat with black poster paint; it'll need two or three coats. Wrap around the red ribbon to form a cheery hatband and put it on Frosty's head. Fray the ends of some patterned ribbon to form a scarf and tie it firmly in place.

Bottles of seasonal liquor make a popular present – but hide such an obvious-looking gift under the decorative guise of a Christmas tree. Find a flower pot just big enough to fit the base of the bottle. From thin cardboard cut out a third section of a large circle and make a deep cone about 3 inches (8cm) shorter than the bottle. Cover the cone with suitable giftwrap.

Put the bottle in the flower pot and place the cone on top. You may need to trim the cone if it seems to cover too much of the flower pot. Double over a piece of tinsel, then tie it in a knot and stick it on top of the "tree."

This heart of woven paper can hold a Valentine's Day gift. Lightweight paper in contrasting colors gives the best effect. Cut a strip of paper 10 by 4 inches (25 by 10cm) and draw the template on page 253 onto it. Cut the shape out and fold it in half. Then cut the two slits as marked on the template. Repeat with another strip of paper in a different color.

Hold a section of the heart in each hand, as shown, with the strips pointing upward. Weave the two sections together, starting with the two inner strips. You need to open out each strip to slot the other strip through it, as illustrated.

A cake, plus candle, is just the right disguise for a birthday present! First, make a drum-shaped frame for the cake: cut a strip of thin cardboard just wider than your gift, then curl it in a circle big enough to cover your gift and stick it in place with sticky tape. Cut a circle to fit as a lid; attach it with strips of tape.

Continue doing this until all the strips are interwoven. It is fairly fiddly but does work; it's clear at this stage why you need lightweight but strong paper! The finished item will open out like a basket, so that it can hold small gifts. The basket would also be very pretty made in felt.

Cut a strip of white paper to cover the sides of the drum and glue it in position. Tuck one edge of the paper under the open end of the drum. Trim the other edge close to the top of the drum to leave a small turning. Cut a series of small nicks in the turning and fold the flaps over, taping them to the lid. Cut a circle slightly smaller than the circumference of the drum and glue it in place.

Place the present inside the cake and put it on a cake stand. Cut two lengths of cord to fit round the circumference of the cake and glue the ends to prevent them from unravelling. Glue one piece to the top of the cake to form "frosting," and the second piece around the bottom, to fix the cake to the stand. Finally, put the candle in a spiked holder and pierce through the center of the cake.

# RED HOT LOVER

A romantic padded heart containing a little gift is perfect to give on Valentine's Day! Cut out two heart shapes from cardboard, one about 1½ inches (4cm) larger all round than the other. From red lining fabric, cut out a heart shape a little bigger than the larger heart. Take a gift box and wrap it in cotton balting. Place it on top of the smaller heart.

When there's enough padding, cover the heart in the red lining, stretching it over the heart shape and sticking it firmly in position on the back with plenty of tape. You'll need to snip the fabric around the inverted point of the heart so that the fabric can open out to fit properly.

Cover the larger heart in white tissue paper. Otherwise, the brown surface may show through the lacey doily. Cut off a frill of about 2 inches (5cm) from the edge of four or five doilies. Pleat them up around the edge of the large heart, fixing them with tape as shown. When the whole heart has been edged like this, apply some strong glue to the middle and place the padded heart in position.

# CONFETTI CLUSTERS

This simple but effective idea is just right for a wedding. Cover your gift with plain paper. Buy some rose petal-shaped confetti. Alternatively, you could make the petals yourself from softly colored tissue paper: fold a piece of tissue into about eight and cut out an oval shape; repeat for as many petals as you need.

Arrange a cluster in a flower-shape on each corner of the gift. Stick each petal into position with a small dab of glue right at one end of the petal. When the glue is dry, bend up the petals to give a 3-dimensional effect. You could use this idea for a silver anniversary gift by wrapping the package in aluminum foil and using petals of just one color.

A gift wrapped up as a prayer book makes an unusual and moving present for a wedding or confirmation. Wrap up the gift in gold paper so that it will look like the closed pages of the book. The last flap should not be folded in the usual way, but should be cut precisely to fit the side of the gift, as shown; glue it in place.

Take two pieces of thick cardboard slightly larger than the size of the gift. You will also need a long strip of thin cardboard measuring the width and length of the gift. Use tape to stick the thick cardboard onto either side of the thin cardboard to make a book cover for the gift. Cover the outside with plain paper, as shown; glue all the edges down firmly.

Spread glue over the inside of the book cover, and place the gift firmly on one side of it. Wrap the cover over the other side of the gift, making sure it's stuck properly. Cut out gold crosses (or other appropriate symbols relevant for your recipient's religion) and stick them in place. This idea is also good for a christening or anniversary gift.

This pretty cradle makes a charming decoration for a baby girl's christening gift. From thin cardboard, cut out a small box shape to make the framework for the crib. Fold up the sides and stick them in place with tape.

Cut a piece of ribbon one and a half times the length of the perimeter of the cot. Sew the ends together to make a loop, and run a gathering thread around the top. Apply some glue to the outside of the box and put the gathered frill over it, positioning it on the lower half. Repeat with more ribbon, sticking the frill over the first one, right at the top edge of the box.

Put some cotton balls, a scrap of lace, and a piece of wide ribbon in the cradle. Take another piece of ribbon, wider than that used for the frills, and cut a strip long enough to make a canopy. Cut a matching strip of cardboard; spread it with glue and cover with the ribbon. Fold it in half and stick in position over one end of the crib.

For the personal touch on Valentine's Day, send a beautiful Valentine's Day card, hand-crafted by you. To make it easier, you can buy the card blanks in most craft stores or stationery suppliers. The designs here are painted on silk. Stretch a piece of white silk over a frame (available from craft stores) and outline the design with gold gutta.

Make sure the gutta lines are continuous so that the paint can't bleed through once the design is painted on. When the gutta is dry, apply the silk colors with a fine brush. Do not be overgenerous with the paint as the silk can only take so much before it is saturated and the colors start to bleed.

When the silk is dry, fix it according to the paint manufacturer's directions. Then glue the silk in position onto the blank card and stick the mount down around it.

Disguise a bottle as a pencil and keep the recipient guessing! Make a cylinder, about 2 inches (5cm) shorter than the bottle, from light cardboard. Join the sides with tape. Draw a third section of a circle – about 3 inches (7.5cm) radius – on pale cardboard and cut it out. Roll it into a cone shape, running the blunt edge of a pair of scissors along it to help it curl. Tape in place.

Make a small cone for the lead of the pencil and glue it onto the larger cone. Attach several lengths of sticky tape to the inside edge of the cone. Putting your arm inside the cylinder, stick the tape down to hold the cone in position. Fit the pencil over the bottle and secure with two strips of tape across the bottom.

Any little girl would be thrilled if her gift looked like a hat. This idea will obviously only work on a gift that is circular and flat, so that the gift itself can form the crown. Cut a brim from a circle of thin cardboard and cover it with a circle of plain, pastel-colored paper. Wrap the present by rolling it in matching paper, as shown.

Make a small gift look that extra bit bigger! Wrap the gift into a ball shape. Cut a strip of paper about three times the width of the gift and long enough to form loops on each side of it. Fold the edges over. Gather small pleats at each end, securing them with sticky tape. Pinch-pleat four gathers in the middle of the strip and secure.

Make sure the paper fits tightly around the base by folding it in a series of small triangles. Trim the turning on the top of the gift to leave a small edge; fold that in neat triangles too. Stick the triangles down onto each other with tape, making sure that the surface is left as flat as possible.

For the trailing sections of the bow, cut a five-sided piece of paper, as shown. Fold over the edges into the center at the back and secure with tape. Gather pinch pleats at one end and secure. At the other end cut out a V-shaped section to form a nicely shaped tail. Repeat the procedure a second time.

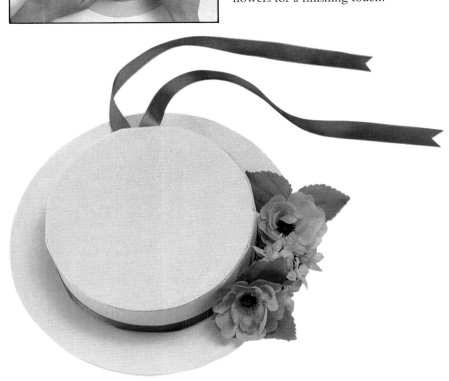

Place the gift in the center of the brim and stick it in position with glue or double-sided tape. Cut another circle of giftwrap slightly smaller than the diameter of the crown; glue it in place. Tie a ribbon around the junction of the crown and brim, leaving the ends trailing. Cut a "V" in the ribbon ends and glue on a couple of artificial flowers for a finishing touch.

Turn the pleated ends of the long strip to the middle to form the loops, and secure with double-sided tape. Stick the tails under the bow with more tape. Finally, put double-sided tape over the join on top of the bow and stick the gift in position. Puff out the loops so they look nice and full.

Cube-shaped gifts will look more interesting disguised as dice – and it's fun if a small, flat gift becomes a domino. For the dice, make sure the gift is a perfect cube by measuring it; the idea won't work well unless it is. Cover the gift with black paper. Then draw several circles on white paper; an easy way of doing this is by tracing the outline of a suitable size of coin.

Cut out the circles carefully and lay them on the box; glue them in place. Look at a real dice to get the juxtaposition of the sides correct. The domino can be treated in the same way.

Brighten up a dull-looking, flat gift by turning it into a playing card. Wrap the gift in plain white paper. Make a template for the spade by folding a piece of paper in half and drawing half the outline against the fold; this way the design will be symmetrical. Trace around the template onto black paper and cut the shape out. Stick the spade in the center of the "card."

Cut two small spades for the corner designs. Then, using a ruler, draw an "A" in two of the corners, being careful to make them both the same. Glue the small spades underneath. Cut a piece of patterned paper – smaller than the card – and stick it on the back. You could vary the idea by making the King or Queen of Hearts for your husband or wife, or the ten of clubs for a ten-year-old.

Here's an attractive way to add sparkle to the Christmas tree. You can buy these plain glass balls from craft suppliers, so look in craft magazines for stockists or try your nearest craft store. As you are decorating a curved surface, it is advisable to keep the design simple. Draw the outlines of your design using a fine multi-purpose felt-tip paint pen.

Try to place the motifs evenly, remembering you will see the far side of the design through the glass ball. Fill in the design with the same color you used for the outlines. You can erase any mistakes with a cloth soaked in turpentine.

Outline your motifs in a contrasting color, combining colors such as red and green, yellow and black, pink and purple. Add tiny dots between the motifs using the same color as that used for the outline. Hang the baubles from your tree with gold giftwrapping thread.

Why not decorate your Christmas gift as if it were a Christmas tree – with glittering baubles and tinsel? Wrap the gift in some elegant paper; something plain but shiny will set off the baubles better than a more complex Christmas design – you could use aluminum foil. Then thread Christmas baubles onto a length of tinsel.

Decide where you want to put the decoration and cover the area with a few strips of double-sided tape. If the package is rectangular, put the baubles in one corner; if the parcel is square, the middle would be better. An upright package like that shown here looks best with the decoration on the top. Group the baubles into a bunch on the gift, wrapping the tinsel around them to form a nest.

201

Holly leaves are an attractive shape and perfect for decorating a festive gift. Measure the length of the diagonal across the top of your package. On a sheet of plain paper draw a large holly leaf, the "vein" of which measures slightly more than half the length of the diagonal.

These Christmas bells ring out merrily from your gift. Make two paper templates, both bell-shaped, with one showing the outline of the clapper from the bottom edge. From thin cardboard, cut out two of each shape.

Trace four holly leaves onto some green cardboard, using the template you have just created. Cut the leaves out and bend them in the middle, creasing them slightly where the central vein would be.

Cover all the cardboard shapes with gold paper (or any color which would coordinate with your giftwrap). Cover both sides, and trim away all the excess paper. On the bell shapes with the clapper, cut a slit from the curved top of the bell to the center of the bell. On the others (the plain ones) cut a slit from the middle of the bottom edge, also to the center.

Make the berries from a ball of cotton wrapped in two squares of red tissue paper. Put a dab of glue inside and twist up the tissue tightly at the base. When the glue is dry, cut off as much excess of the twist as possible. Group the leaves and berries on the package; attach with glue or double-sided tape.

Pierce a hole in the top of the plain bell shapes and thread them with a length of ribbon. Then slot the pairs of bell shapes together (i.e., the plain one, and the one with the clapper) so that they form three-dimensional shapes, as shown here. Tie a group of as many bells as you like onto your gift. This idea can also be used for decorating a wedding gift.

# SPRING CHICK

This cheery chick will brighten up any Easter gift. Cut out two cardboard circles the same size. Then cut a small circle from the center of each to create two wide rings. Put both rings together and wind yellow yarn around them, passing the yarn through the center. Continue doing this until the rings are well covered and the inner circle is almost full of yarn.

Snip through all the yarn along the outer edge of the cardboard rings. Pass a length of yarn between the two rings. Wind it tightly around all the strands of yarn and tie it firmly, leaving long ends. Cut off the cardboard circles and fluff out the ball. Make a bigger ball for the body from two larger rings. Before cutting, pass a pipe cleaner through the rings to form the legs.

Tie the two balls together firmly. Bend the "legs" up at the ends and wind a section of pipe cleaner around each foot, leaving a V-shape on either side so that each foot now has three "claws." Paint the feet and legs red. Make eyes and a beak out of felt, then glue into position. This would work just as well with a Christmas robin decoration, using red and brown wool.

# YOUR NUMBER'S UP

Paste the recipient's age in a great big number on the side of their gift so that *everybody* knows how old they are! Draw around the gift, so that you know exactly what size the numbers must be to fill the side of the gift and make a big impact.

Draw the appropriate number using a ruler and measure carefully. Choose thin cardboard or plain paper in a contrasting color to the giftwrap.

Cut the numbers out and stick them in position on your gift. You could make a numerical tag to match. This idea could be adapted for use with gifts celebrating wedding anniversaries – 25, 50, and so on.

Disguise the unmistakable shape of a record by making it look like a cushion. First create paper tassels. Cut a piece of colored paper into narrow strips, leaving about 1 inch (2.5cm) at the bottom uncut so that you create a fringe. Roll up the fringe, catching in a short length of narrow ribbon. Secure the tassel with colored tape.

Take some giftwrap that is more than twice the size of the gift. Fold it in half around the record and cut it so that it is just a little larger. Join two of the sides together with colored tape along their full length, attaching the ends of the tassels at the corners as you do so. Put a strip of tape over the folded edge of the "bag."

Stuff the inside of the "bag" on both sides of the disk with shredded tissue, being careful to put some in the corners. Don't use too much or the giftwrap will wrinkle. Seal along the remaining open edge with tape.

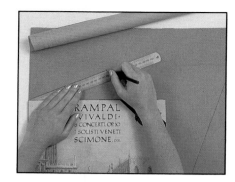

Here's another clever idea for disguising a record. Take two large squares of cardboard; the side of a box will do. Position the record in one corner as shown and draw a line from the bottom right corner of the record to the top right corner of the cardboard. Draw a second rule from the top left corner of the record to complete the kite shape. Repeat for the other square.

Cut out the shapes and sandwich the record between them. Cover one side in colored paper, folding over the edges and fixing them with sticky tape on the reverse. Cut another piece of paper slightly smaller than the cardboard shape. Glue it in position on the back of the kite.

Draw two lines joining the four corners of the kite, and put contrasting tape along them; take care not to stretch the tape as it will pucker the paper. Cut out as many paper bow shapes as you want for the kite's tail. Attach the bows with double-sided tape or glue to a length of ribbon. Then stick the tail in position behind the longest point of the kite.

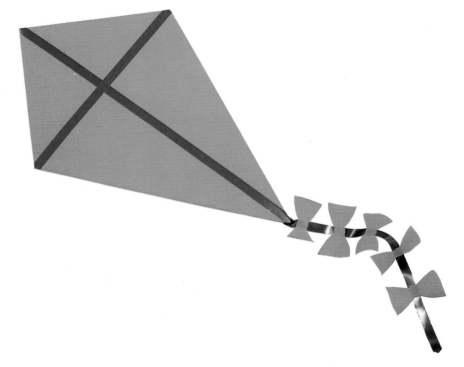

# STENCILED GIFT BOXES

Decorate some pretty boxes with stencils and stencil crayons. You can either buy the stencils from a craft store or make your own. Position the stencil over the box lid and tape it firmly in place. Now rub a little stencil crayon onto one corner of the film. Pick up some color with a stencil brush and apply it to the stencil cut-out with a circular motion, starting at the edge and working inward.

Once you have finished the first color, change stencils and apply the second color. Use a clean brush at this stage or your colors will appear muddy.

After you have completed the lid, stencil the sides of the box. Be sure to tape the film firmly in position to stop it from slipping.

# EASTER BASKET

Fill this pretty basket with tiny sweet eggs to delight a child at Easter. Using the templates on page 244, cut out two sides and a base in pale blue cardboard and the grass in green gummed paper. Lightly score the sides of the baskets along the broken lines with a craft knife. Then stick on the grass.

Fold the sides backward along the scored lines and join end to end in a ring by gluing each end tab under the opposite end of the other side. Glue the base under the base tabs. Cut a strip of pale blue cardboard for the handle measuring 12 by ⅜ inch (30 by 1cm). Stick the ends inside the basket.

Cut out two rabbits in brown cardboard. Glue a ball of cotton to the rabbits as bobtails. Cut two strips of pale blue cardboard 1½ by ⅜ inch (4 by 1cm). Fold them widthwise in half to make hinges. Glue one half to the back of the rabbit, matching the fold to the broken line. Glue the other half to the basket under the handles.

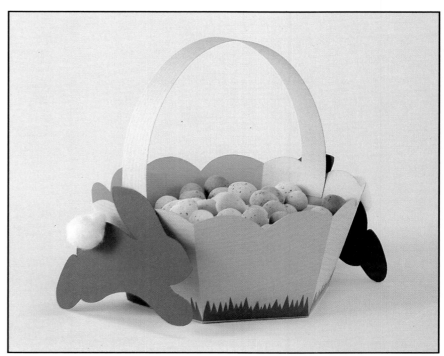

# POTPOURRI CONE

Fill this pretty cone with potpourri and let the scent waft through your home. Draw a 12 inches (30cm) diameter semi-circle with a compass on a piece of mottled peach-colored paper. Cut it out and bend into the cone shape. Cut away a slice so that the ends overlap smoothly, then glue the overlapped ends together. Leave to dry.

Cut out motifs from a white paper doily and stick to the cone with spray glue. Coat the cone all over with polyvinyl acetate (PVA) medium. Set aside until the medium has hardened and become clear. Then apply two more coats.

Cut a strip of paper 10 by ⅝ inch (25 by 1.5cm) for the handle. Glue the ends inside the cone and coat with the PVA medium. Hang the handle over a door handle to dry. Tie ribbons in a bow and glue to the cone below the handle.

# PAISLEY POUCH

Use a sophisticated print like a Paisley design to set off this pouch which is ideal for holding a small gift. Apply giftwrap to one side of thin cardboard with spray glue. Use the template on page 244 to cut out two pouches. Mark the position of the holes and broken lines. Cut the tabs off one pouch and punch holes on the other one.

Score both pouches along the broken lines on the right side. Fold the tabs backward. Stick the pouches together with double-sided tape on the tabs.

Thread cord through the holes and knot the ends inside. To close the pouch, hold the sides between your thumb and finger and gently squeeze the pouch open. Now press down one of the ellipses. Close the other ellipse on top.

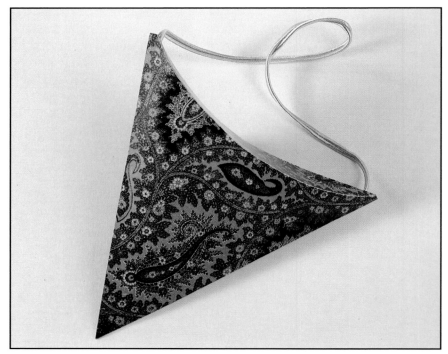

# GREETING CARDS

# COCKTAIL GLASSES

# PUFFINS

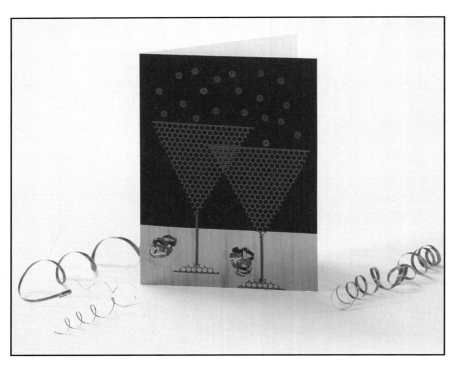

Colorful puffins, cut from a sheet of giftwrap, keep a lookout from their perch. Cut card 18 by 5¼ inches (28 by 13cm). The card is blue on the inside and white on the outside. On the outside, from the left, score 3½ inches (9cm) and 7½ inches (19cm) across and fold. Turn the card over and on the inside, from the left, score and fold 8 inches (20cm) across.

Cut out three puffins and spray glue the first onto the outside of the far right-hand panel of card, facing right. Cut round him with a craft knife, leaving him attached by his tail. The score line on the outside will let him stand forward.

This card, in party mood, could be used for a birthday, an engagement, or for congratulations. Cut a piece of purple glossy card 8 by 12 inches (20 by 30cm). Score a fold down the center of the card (6 inches/ 15cm across). Cut two triangular shapes and bases from pink sequin waste and a piece of iridescent film to fit the width of the card. Mark with pencil dots where the glasses should be placed.

Glue the other two puffins in place on the inside. Any giftwrap with a distinct animal motif can be used in this way to make a striking card.

Using a spray booth, spray glue onto the back of the iridescent "table" and smooth down to remove creases. Trim away any excess. Spray glue onto the back of cocktail glasses and position on the dot marks. Spray the bases at the same time.

With a rubber-based glue, stick down strips of very narrow ribbon for the stems, then stick down the bases. Curl two narrow pieces of ribbon, and place sequin "bubbles" over the glasses. A pair of tweezers will make this an easier task. Glue curls of ribbon on the "table" and leave for a few minutes for the glue to set. Any residue may be gently rubbed away when dry.

A teenage motif badge for sewing onto jeans and jackets makes a card and gift – it can be carefully peeled off the card at a later date and sewn onto a favorite garment. To put the pop singer in the spotlight, cut glossy red card 6 by 8½ inches (15 by 22cm). Score and fold 4¼ inches (11cm). Draw a spotlight shape on silver paper or plastic film using a ruler.

Cut out with a craft knife and trim the curve with a pair of small scissors.

The bouquet on this bright and cheerful greeting card is made up of colored gummed paper squares torn into simple shapes. Cut a rectangle of white cardboard measuring 15 by 10 inches (38 by 25cm). Score across the center widthwise using a craft knife. Fold the card in half along the scored line.

First glue down the spotlight and trim any overhang on the edge of the card. Stick down the pop singer with rubber-based glue and hold firmly in place for a minute or two until the glue dries. The disks on the main picture are buttons purchased from a specialty button store.

All the shapes have straight edges. Press a ruler down a gummed square, then lift one edge of paper and pull it up against the ruler to tear it neatly. Now tear across the paper again either diagonally or straight across to form the various shapes.

Arrange the pieces on the front of the card within a border of narrow strips and squares. Moisten the back of the gummed pieces to stick them in position.

This small piece of quilting is from a ready-printed panel. It will shrink a little when it has been quilted, so measure and cut the window from card *after* you have finished the piece. You will need very thin batting to back the cotton panel. Cut a piece of card 18 by 6 inches (45 by 15cm) and score two folds 6 inches (15cm) apart. Pin the panel to a slightly larger square of batting.

On a larger piece of work, muslin would be used as a backing fabric, but in this instance it has been left out so that there is less bulk inside the card. Working from the center, baste the two layers together, making sure the picture covers the batting.

Cotton thread gives best results in hand-quilting. Starting from the center, with a knot on the back, sew with tiny running stitches. Finish the thread with a double backstitch. Take out the basting stitches or you will lose the quilted effect. Measure the finished piece and cut a window from the center of the 3–fold card. With double-sided tape, stick down the quilted panel and back flap of the card.

A window box full of spring flowers is sure to bring cheer. Here a ready-cut, 3–fold card with a window is used. Fold under the left-hand side of the card (looking from the inside), marked with a cross in the second picture. With a sharp pencil, draw through the window outline and cut out a second window using a craft knife and steel ruler.

Place ½ inch (1cm) of double-sided sticky tape around the center window and edges of the card. Cut a piece of *broderie anglaise* and a piece of tracing paper cut slightly larger than the aperture. Peel off the tape backing and stick down the curtain, then the tracing paper. Peel off the tape backing on the edges of card and close the left-hand side over. Light will filter through.

Apply "stick-on" flowers (purchased on a strip) in a line, half on the card and half on the tracing paper. Finish with a strip of satin ribbon or paper for the window box. Add a couple more flowers to the top of the window if you wish.

This top dog with a smart plaid bow makes a great greeting card. Cut out a cardboard pattern of the template on page 244 and mark the broken lines. Place the pattern on an 8 inch (20cm) square of blue cardboard with the lower edges level and the dog's nose against one edge. Draw around the pattern. Score along the broken lines and cut along solid lines.

Here is a card that will appeal to cat lovers everywhere. Cut a rectangle of colored cardboard 10¼ by 7¾ inches (26 by 6.5cm). Use the template on page 244 to draw the design on the right-hand side of the card. Score along the broken lines with a craft knife. Cut out the long window edge, window panes, cat's eye, and the edge of the windowsill.

Fold the card in two along the scored line and trace around the dog on the lower section of the card. Now cut out this dog, leaving the fold intact and cutting away the base of the tail on a neat curve.

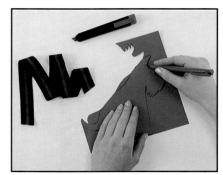

Fold the card in half along the scored line and then open out the inside of the card. Cut a rectangle of pretty giftwrap measuring 43.4 by 2½ inches (12 by 6.5cm). Glue the paper inside the card over the top window panes.

With the card opened out flat, peel the backing off a square of black, flocked, sticky-backed plastic and press onto the card. Turn the card over and cut around the two dogs. Fold the card in half and glue a ribbon bow to the front.

Cut out card 10 by 5½ inches (25 by 14cm). Score and fold 5 inches (12.5cm) across. Trace out the fish on the smooth side of fusible web. Cut out the fish just outside the pencil outline and place the rough side of web onto the back of your fabric. Press with a warm iron to melt the glue. Cut out on the outline. Peel off the backing and position on the card. Press with a dry iron.

Diagonal lines of spotted ribbon and self-adhesive labels give this card a "dotty" air. Cut a piece of black card 10 by 6¼ inch (25 by 16cm). Score across, then fold 5 inches (12.5cm). On the inside top left-hand corner measure 1½ inches (4cm) along the top of the card and down the side edge. Mark with dots and score. Fold the corner back to the outside of the card.

Draw in the eyes and details of the fish with felt-tip pens. Alternatively, you can use sequins for the eyes. Cut rocks and stick down in place with spray glue.

Rule a diagonal line across the front of the card from top left to bottom right. Measure and cut ribbons to fit either side of this line. Cut them slightly longer, to be trimmed later. Cut a triangle of ribbon to fit behind the turned-down corner. Spray the backs of the ribbon with glue in a spray booth. Place in position, then smooth down and trim the edges.

Cut sea and sand from organza and stick on the card with spray glue. Trim the edges with a craft knife and use offcuts to make sea ripples and waves. Note: Be sure to use card of at least 160 pounds/square inch (240gsm) or the heat of the iron will distort it.

On the front bottom left-hand corner of the card, stick on self-adhesive dots and also on the folded-over, top right-hand corner.

A favorite Victorian pastime was to make greeting cards from printed "scraps." Cut a piece of cardboard 16½ by 10 inches (42 by 25cm) and score across the center widthwise. Fold the card in half. Cut out a large heart from mottled pink paper and glue it to the middle of the card.

Cut out sprays of flowers from reproductions of sheets of Victorian scraps, available at craft stores and some museums. Alternatively, use pictures from seed catalogs. Arrange the flowers along the edge of the heart and when you are happy with the design, glue them in place. Glue on single flowers to fill any gaps in between.

Highlight the flowers with a fine gold pen. Use a thick gold pen to draw a line ¾ inch (2cm) from the ends of the card. Cut two ⅝ inch (1.5cm) wide strips of marbled paper and glue along the ends of the card with spray glue. To finish, stick a butterfly or other motif in one corner.

Offcuts of shot silk or other fabrics are woven into a landscape of green fields, hedges, yellow corn, blue sky, and pink evening sunset. A ready-cut, 3–fold card was used. Mark the top left-hand corner inside the card with a pencil cross. Cut canvas about 4 inches (10cm) square. Lay the card with oval aperture over the canvas and mark the edges lightly. Rule a square just outside these marks.

Cut strips of fabric approximately ½ inch (1cm) wide and 5 inches (12.5cm) long. Do not worry if they fray as this adds to the charm. Thread a large tapestry needle, and starting from the bottom, weave green strips. Continue with yellow fields, hedges, and sky.

Attach double-sided tape around the oval window and along three sides of the panel, as shown. Trim canvas ¼ inch (6mm) outside the ruled square and peel off the backing from double-sided tape. Stick the canvas in place and close the card – the left side with the cross is the side to fold in. Smooth from the folded edge to the outside so that the card stays flat.

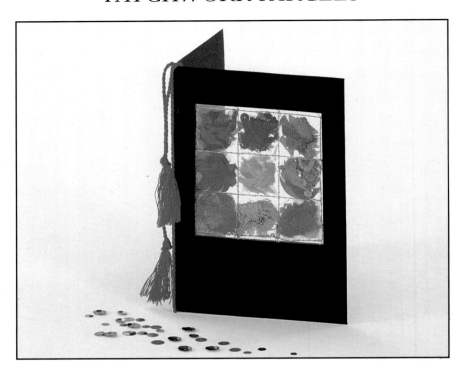

Windows open to reveal flowers cut from giftwrap which could also wrap the gift. Cut glossy green card 8½ by 6 inches (22 by 15cm). Score and fold 4¼ inches (11cm). Cut a 1½ inch (4cm) equilateral triangle template. Open the card flat and on the inside front draw four triangles. With a steel ruler and craft knife cut two sides of triangles and score the third.

Cut a piece of white paper the same size as the closed card and lay it under the card front. Open up the windows and draw the triangles through the windows. These will be your guides for sticking on the pieces of flowered paper. Mark the top left-hand corner of the inside of the card and paper with a cross. Cut out four triangles of flowers.

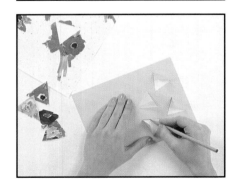

Glue flower triangles on the paper where marked in pencil. Place a line of glue along all four edges on the front of the paper and attach it face down on the inside front of the card. Open up the windows and you will see peeping flowers.

Cut nine heaps of lurex, silk, and satin. Cut two pieces of acetate film 4 inches (10cm) and 3¼ inches (9.5cm). Draw a 3 inch (7.5cm) grid of 1 inch (2.5cm) squares with a Chinagraph pencil. Use polyester thread and machine two center horizontal lines and a lefthand vertical. Stuff the center square. Machine a right vertical to close the center square. Stuff the squares on the left, top, and bottom center.

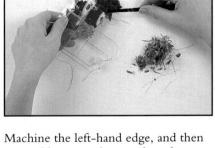

Machine the left-hand edge, and then top and bottom edges to close the squares. Stuff three right-hand squares and machine the right-hand edge to close. Pull threads to the back and knot. Trim and put a dot of glue on each knot to hold it.

Make or buy a 3–fold card and cut a double window mount (see page 210). Mark the inside top left-hand corner with a pencil cross. Put double-sided tape around the center window of card and the edges. Pull off the backing tape and place patchwork parcels in the window. Close the card and add cord and tassel.

K ites flying in a high spring sky are always a cheerful sight and these three are made from giftwrap and narrow satin ribbon. Cut pale blue card 8½ by 6 inches (22 by 15cm). Score 4¼ inches (11cm) across, then fold. Cut out kites in three different sizes and papers using a ruler. Arrange and stick on the card using spray glue.

Cut narrow satin ribbons slightly longer than the card so they will hang below the bottom of the card. Cut short lengths of ribbon for bows.

A theme card to give to a musical friend. The treble clefs are buttons. Cut red glossy card 8½ by 6 inches (22 by 15cm). Score 4¼ inches (11cm) across, then fold. Draw a square 2¼ by 3 inches (5.5 by 7.5cm) on white paper. Rule two staves – groups of five lines ⅛ inch (3mm) apart – using a fine black felt-tip pen. Cut out the square.

Glue and hold in place for a moment since satin ribbon tends to resist glue at first. Some of the bows can be a "V" of twisted ribbon.

Center the square of music paper on card so that you have an equal margin on three sides. Visually, it is better to have a larger margin at the base of the card. Mark the corners of music lightly on the card and stick down using spray glue. Place the opened card on a piece of felt and pierce two holes for the buttons, using dividers or a thick needle.

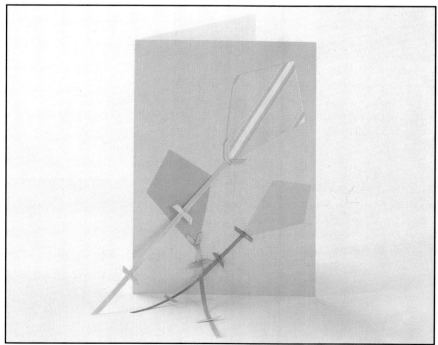

From the back, sew on buttons through the holes you have pierced. Then knot the thread and trim. Finish knots with a dab of glue.

Using mono thread "lockweave" needlepoint canvas 10 holes to 1 inch or 8 holes to 1cm, cut 7 by 5½ inches (18 by 14cm). Find the center of the canvas and mark a center hole on four sides. Draw two crosses in different colors on either side of the center and side holes. Without counting the center hole, count 29 holes either side lengthwise. Rule a border line.

You will find a chart to follow on page 251. Thread a tapestry needle with either double-knitting yarn or tapestry yarn. Counting holes, work long stitch in the pale lilac color first.

Continue working toward the center, finishing the four corners last. Cut a 3-fold card 18 by 8 inches (45 by 20cm). Score and fold at 6 inch (15cm) intervals. Measure the finished piece and cut a slightly smaller window in the center panel of the card. Trim canvas to ¼ inch (6mm) all round and mount using double-sided tape. Close the card and stick down.

Cut card into a 8½ inch (22cm) square. Center your compass point horizontally 2 inches (5.5cm) from the top of the card. Draw an arc so that it touches the sides and top edge of the card, then cut through both thicknesses. You could make a template of this shape if you wanted to make several cards.

Brightly colored origami paper is perfect for this exuberant card. Either draw on the back of paper or cut freehand a collection of shapes and colors.

Arrange paper shapes in the order of gluing and stick them onto the card. Tweezers will help you to apply glue to the tiny star shapes, not your fingers!

A detachable finger puppet of a jolly circus clown will delight a child. Cut card 7 by 10 inches (18 by 25cm). Score 5 inches (12.5cm) across, then mark 2¼ inches (5.5cm) down the sides of the folded card. Measure across the top 2¼ inches (6cm) and mark. Cut through both thicknesses of card to form the apex of a "marquee." Draw the roof of the marquee. Cut a "stand" for the puppet.

Just the card to please a young girl who dreams of becoming a ballet dancer. Cut card 12 by 6 inches (30 by 15cm) Score 6 inches (15cm) across then fold. Cut the skirt from a piece of net 12 by 3 inches (30 by 7.5cm). Fold in half down its length and press with a warm iron. Sew, with small running stitches, along this fold. Make a double stitch to start, then gather tightly and finish with a double stitch.

Trace out templates 10, 11, and 12 on page 248 and transfer onto thin card to make your own templates. Cut out two balloons from card and satin ribbon strings. Using turquoise felt, cut two hats, two hands, and a bowtie. Cut two heads from white felt, and two circles, one for his nose and one for his hat, from pink felt. Cut eyes from narrow black satin ribbon.

Use marbled paper for the background. Cut 5 inches (13cm) square. Cut the mirror from silver paper or foil. Details of how to draw a curve are given on page 216. Cut the bodice from satin and straps from satin ribbon.

Glue the balloons and ribbons in place. Sandwich the clown's hands between the two pieces of felt for the head, holding in place with a dab of glue. Sew, with a running stitch, round the clown's head. Glue on the hat, bobble, eyes, nose, and bowtie. Place the clown on the stand and he will appear to be holding the balloons.

Center the background paper and attach with spray glue. Then glue the bodice and mirror. The straps will be easier to put on with rubber-based glue. Mark where the skirt is to be attached and pierce two holes each side with dividers. Sew from the back of the card, then tie a knot and dab with glue. Make two more holes in the same way for the ballet shoes pin. Finish with a silver star.

# BOYS AND GIRLS COME OUT TO PLAY

Cut card 12 by 5 inches (30 by 13cm). Score 6 inches (15cm) across, then fold. With the fold on top, find the center and mark with a pencil dot. Measure down 2½ inches (6cm) on each side. Rule a line from each side point to the middle mark to form the roof. Stick down ribbon forming a miter at the apex of the roof. Cut two pieces of medium weight giftwrap 8 by 3 inches (20 by 7.5cm).

Trace out templates 14 and 15 on page 248. Fold a length of giftwrap in half, then in half twice more. Draw on half a boy or girl, making sure hands are on folds. Cut out. When you draw the second child, check the folds are in the opposite direction, so that when they are opened they are the left and right of the card. Open out boys and girls, then refold alternate ways.

From green and pink paper cut out a boy and girl. Glue them to the blank side of the folded figures. Glue the last girl and boy to the card so that their feet are on the bottom edge. Fold figures flat to fit in an envelope.

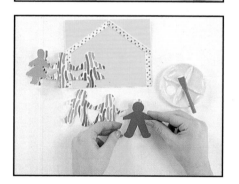

# BIRTHDAY BALLOONS

Cut yellow card 8½ by 12¾ inches (22 by 33cm). Score and fold 4¼ inches (11cm) and 8½ inches (22cm). Trace template 13 on page 248, and transfer to card to make a template. Place over folded card, then mark around the balloon outline at the top and cut through all three thicknesses. Open out the card. Trace balloon shapes onto the center panel and cut.

Place double-sided tape around the balloon holes on the inside center of the card. Cut small pieces of narrow ribbon and stick across the neck of the balloons. Using the balloon template, cut three satin balloons slightly larger. Remove double-sided backing and stick them in place. Stick down the left side of the 3–fold card using double-sided tape.

Cut three "reflection" squares out of white or silver fabric and glue onto the three balloons. Cut four lengths of narrow ribbon, one shorter, so that it will appear to pass behind the red balloon. Using a sharp pencil, rule guide lines for where the ribbons will be placed. Glue them down, and leave for a minute or two for the glue to dry. Then trim the ends.

O ur mischievous black cat seems not to have noticed the little mouse! Cut card 9 by 7 inches (23 by 18cm). Score 4½ inches (11.5cm) across and fold along top of card. Trace cat templates 16–21 on page 248 and transfer onto thin card to make your own templates. Draw around pieces onto black paper or card. Keep paws and tail the right way round.

C ut card 12 by 8 inches (30 by 20cm), score and fold 6 inches (15cm) across. Trace out templates 22–25 on page 248. Transfer the designs onto thin card to make your own templates. Cut out from thin card two arms, two legs, the head, and body. From brown felt cut out the same pieces, but slightly larger. Glue the felt to card – make a left and right leg. When glue is dry, trim the edges.

Cut out a black cat, a tree shape from tissue paper or card, and two green eyes. Mark with a sharp pencil where the pieces will fit on the card. Stick on in order using spray glue: the tree, body, paws, tail, ears, and eyes.

Tear green tissue paper to resemble hills and hedges and cut gingham tablecloth. Glue them to card and position "stick-on" flowers. Glue on Teddy's head and punch holes in the body, arms, and legs. Mark shoulder holes on card, since Teddy will be attached through them. Punch or cut out with a cross, so that brass paperclips will pass through.

Use stationers' self-adhesive dots for the cat's nose and pupils. Finish by drawing whiskers using white Chinagraph pencil. Draw around limbs and ears with a soft pencil to make the cat stand out.

Join Teddy's legs to his body with brass paperclips. Pass paperclips through holes at the top of the arms, body, and card, then open out on the back to secure him. Glue on small black beads for eyes and nose. With a fine felt-tip pen, draw in his snout and mouth.

The card is a store-bought 3–fold with window. Cut out a circle in the left-hand section to match the window (see page 210). Trace out template 35 on page 249. Put masking tape in each corner to hold the tracing still. Then place silk over the tracing, holding it firm with masking tape. Trace through onto silk using a soft pencil.

Cut glossy red card 7 by 9 inches (18 by 23cm), score and fold 4½ inches (11.5cm) across. Cut on the bias four strips of Christmas fabrics 1 by 12 inches (2.5 by 30cm) long. Fold strips lengthwise, then machine ⅛ inch (3mm) seam allowance. Leaving a length of thread at end, thread a bodkin and knot. Thread bodkin back through the tube with damp fingers.

Place silk in an embroidery frame and draw over the lines of design with gutta. This will stop the silk paints from running into each other. Leave to dry thoroughly – it may take an hour. A hair drier will speed up the process.

Thread a length of double knitting yarn through each tube. Pin ends of tubes to a firm surface. Braid by laying four strands over the left hand, then take left strand over two middle strands and right strand over one. Continue to the end. Ease into a circle, then cross over ends and sew through to secure. Trim and finish with a bow.

Shake or stir the fabric paints. Using a clean damp brush, flood each petal area with paint in one swift stroke. When paint is dry, place a piece of fabric under the silk and iron on the wrong side for 2 minutes to set paint. Wash out gutta from silk and dry if you wish. Trim to just larger than the window. Stick down the fabric and left-hand card section with double-sided tape.

Bind trimmed ends with embroidery cotton. Tie, then knot and trim. Draw an arched border (see page 216) using a gold pen. Center the finished wreath and pierce through card with a thick needle or point of dividers. Sew through from back of card and knot thread. Trim and finish with a dot of glue to hold firm.

A bunch of golden roses to celebrate 50 golden years together. Cut card 6½ by 10 inches (16.5 by 25cm). Score and fold 5 inches (12.5cm). Find the horizontal center of the card and draw a circle with gold pen taped to compass. Cut three 4 inch (10cm) pieces of gold giftwrap ribbon and cut ends diagonally to use as leaves.

Arrange gold roses with leaves and hold in place by binding together with fine wire. Cut a piece of gold paper in a triangle shape, curving the top.

On red fabric draw in pencil four 3½ inch (9cm) squares and cut out. Fold in a ¼ inch (6mm) seam allowance and press. Find the center of the square by folding diagonally each way and mark with tip of iron. Fold down one corner to this mark and pin. Continue with other corners to make a square. Catch center points with a small stitch. Fold in again and sew. Complete all four squares.

Wrap paper around flowers and glue at the back to secure. You may like to put a dab of glue to hold roses in place. Apply glue to back of bunch of flowers and stick in place on card. Add golden birds and hearts and a large "50" cake decoration.

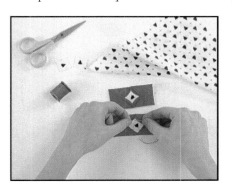

Cut four ¾ inch (2cm) squares from fir-tree fabric. Place two red squares right sides together and sew down one side to make a double square. Pin a fir-tree patch diagonally over the seam on the right side and curl back the folded edges surrounding the patch. Slipstitch to hold in place. Repeat to make another double square.

Sew the double squares together and place third and fourth fir-tree patches over seams. Sew tiny beads in corners of "windows." Cut card 10 by 7 inches (25 by 18cm). Score and fold 5 inches (12.5cm). Mark top center and sides 2½ inches (6cm) down with pencil. Cut through card to form a point. Glue the finished square, centered horizontally, onto card. Add gold border.

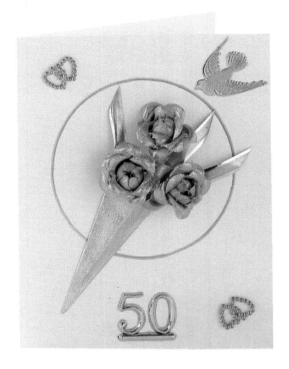

# CANDLELIT CHRISTMAS TREE

Cut card 6 by 8 inches (15 by 20cm) and score down center. Trace template 32 on page 249. Transfer onto thin card and draw round on green paper. Cut out using the craft knife. Set your sewing machine to a fairly wide satin stitch. Sew, moving card from side to side to form garlands. Pull threads through to the back. Tie off with knot and finish with dab of glue.

Stick on self-adhesive spots to resemble Christmas tree balls. Cut narrow satin ribbon into 14 ½ inch (1cm) pieces.

Glue them in place at end of the branches on the back of the card. Tweezers will help you to hold them steady. Leave until glue dries. Cut tops diagonally to look like candles. Add the finishing touch – a red star on top of the tree.

# THE FRIENDLY SNOWMAN

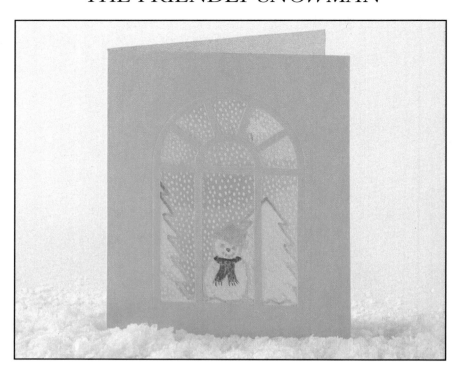

The snowman at the window invites us to come outside to play in the snow. Cut off the left-hand side of this 3–fold card so that light will shine through the window. Cut a piece of film slightly smaller than the folded card. Draw snowman and trees onto paper to fit between window bars. Place paper under film, and on the right side draw the outline of the snowman and trees.

Turn over film and color in the trees and snowman using a white Chinagraph pencil.

Turn back film onto the right side and draw in a scarf and nose with a red Chinagraph pencil. Add face details in silver. Attach film to the inside of the card with double-sided tape and place a silver star where it can be seen shining through the window.

222

A simple, easily made card in unusual colors for Christmas. Cut card 11 on page 248 by 4¼ by 8 inches (11 by 20cm). Score and fold 4 inch (10cm). The fold is at the top of card. Cut a strip of green plastic from an old shopping bag. Tear four strips of tissue in shades of orange and yellow. The fir-tree is from a strip of self-adhesive "stickers."

Cut card 9 by 7 inches (23 by 18cm), score 4½ inches (11.5cm) and fold along top. Trace template 33 on page 249 and transfer onto thin card to make a template. Place on polystyrene wallpaper and draw round with a soft pencil. Cut out with craft knife. Cut out ice caps and ground from iridescent plastic or silver paper.

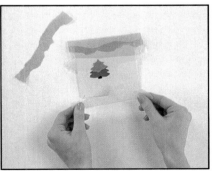

Arrange strips so that colors overlap and produce new colors and tones. Stick down the tree. Spray glue onto the back of strips and stick down.

Glue down mountains, ground, and polar bear, placing the latter in front of the peaks. Glue on silver sequin stars.

Trim excess paper from edges of card with a steel ruler and sharp craft knife.

With a silver pen, draw in the polar bear's features: legs, paws, and ears. The polar bear could also be made from white felt.

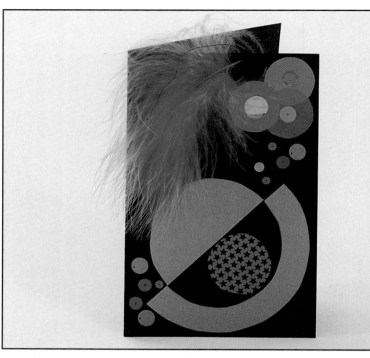

Cut card 6 by 8½ inches (15 by 22cm). Score and fold 4¼ inches (11cm) along top. Mark the center top of the card with a pencil dot. Cut a triangle from sequin waste. Place on card and mark two sides at the bottom of the tree. Glue along edges of tree and hold in place on card until glue dries. Any residue glue can be rubbed away when dry.

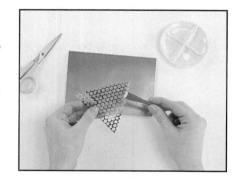

Cut a base for the tree from a piece of card or paper. Curl over scissors a number of narrow pieces of ribbon cut about 3¼ inches (9.5cm) long.

The attraction of this card lies in combining circles cut from a variety of materials of a single color. The feather adds a final touch of frivolity. Cut card 9 by 7 inches (23 by 18cm). Score and fold 4½ inches (11.5cm). Find sequins of different sizes but similar colors, and also paper, sequin waste, satin paper, and foil. Sequin waste can be marked with dividers.

Draw circles of different sizes on your chosen materials. Any round objects can be used for this, or use a pair of compasses. Cut out.

Glue on base and add sequin star to top of tree. Slip curled ribbons through every other hole in sequin waste and every other row, starting at top of tree. No need to tie them; they will stay in place.

Position circles and sequins to make an interesting arrangement and glue in place. Finally glue on a feather of matching color.

# NEW YEAR'S DOVE

A dove of peace for New Year's. It is made from a paper doily with calendar dates falling from its beak. Cut deep blue card 12 by 8 inches (30 by 20cm). Score 6 inches (15cm) and fold. Draw freehand two curves at top of card to represent clouds and cut with craft knife.

Trace dove template 34 on page 249 and transfer to thin card to make your own template. Trace dove onto white paper doily and cut out, together with dates 1 and 31 from an old calendar and a strip of translucent film waved along the upper edge to resemble hills.

Spray glue all pieces and place on the card together with four star sequins. Using a silver pen, draw a line along the edge of the cloud curves.

# WINTER TOWNSCAPE

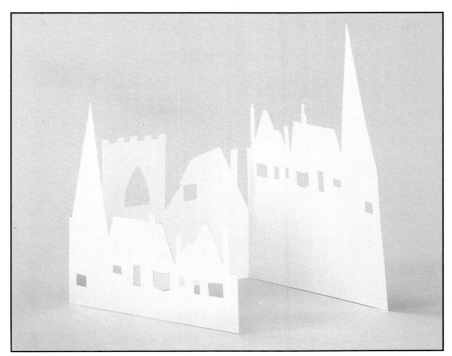

This card could be used for the New Year's or Christmas. You will see from template 31 on page 249 that only two sides of the 3–sided card are shown. The left-hand portion is a repeat of the right but with 2¾ inches (7cm) added to the bottom, so it stands taller. Trace the template, adding an extra section to make the left-hand part of the card. Rub soft pencil over back of tracing.

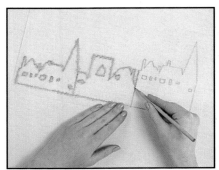

Cut a piece of white card 13 by 6 inches (33 by 15cm). Lay tracing over, right side up, lining up the lower edges. Hold in place with masking tape and draw over outline to transfer drawing.

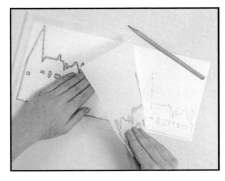

Use a ruler to help keep lines straight and cut out. Score and fold into sections. Trim lower edge and 1/16 inch (1mm) from one side of the card so that it will hold flat. You will need an extra piece of card in the envelope to protect the points.

Cut card 8½ by 6 inches (22 by 15cm), score and fold 4¼ inches (11cm). Trace out heart 37 on page 250 and transfer to a thin piece of card to make your own template. Cut out a heart in thin white card. Place the template on the front of the card at a slight angle and draw round in pencil. Cut round pencil line, leaving enough uncut at the bottom to enable the card to stand.

Glue dried flower petals onto a white heart working in rows from the outside to the center. Use a rubber-based glue; tweezers will help to hold petals steady. Finish with a whole flower in the center.

Cut a border from a paper doily. Spread a thin line of glue on the outside of the main card heart. Pleat doily border on to the glue all round the heart. Stick petal heart over pleated doily. Cover with a piece of clean paper and smooth down. Hold for a minute until glue dries. Lastly stick on Victorian angel motif on top right-hand corner of card.

Capture the hosts of the party on a roll of film to make personal invitation cards, each one a little different. The children were delighted to be involved, especially when they opened the "gifts," even though these were empty boxes!

Make a mask to fit the "sunken plate" area of the card mount and mark the corners of photographs with a compass or sharp pencil point. Cut the photograph with a sharp craft knife and ruler and use spray glue to affix.

Invitations can be handmade by children too – a great way to keep them happy and involved in party planning. This rabbit is for an Easter football party given by a nine-year old boy. He drew the picture, then photocopied it a number of times. Each invitation can be hand-colored before being glued to cards.

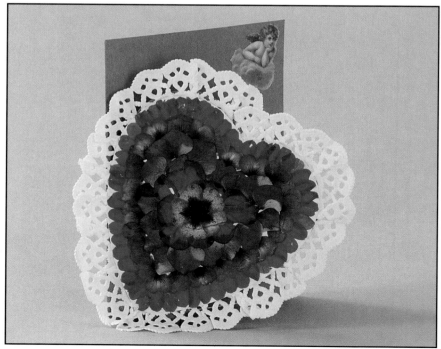

Use a mold from a cake decorating shop and fill it with tiny cake candies. Cut a 3–fold card 16½ by 7½ inches (42 by 19cm). Score and fold 5½ inches (14cm). Tape heart to the back of the tracing paper. Turn over and rub along the edge of the heart to make a template. Line up heart tracing in the center of the middle section of card and transfer outline. Cut out.

Place double-sided tape round heart aperture and around edges of the left-hand portion of card, marked with a cross. Remove backing from tape around the heart and place mold in position. Press to stick firmly. Put narrow line of double-sided tape around edge of heart.

Pour candies into the heart until full and pack out with a piece of batting cut to heart shape. Take off backing from tape around heart and from left-hand portion of card. Fold over card and press down. A pretty pink bow is the finishing touch.

A doll's straw bonnet forms the basis of this card and is decorated with spring-colored ribbons, flowers and a butterfly. Cut card 6 by 8½ inches (15 by 22cm). Score and fold 4¼ inches (11cm). Cut length of yellow ribbon and cut inverted "V" shape at ends. Hold in place around hat and sew, leaving tails at center back. Repeat with a length of slightly narrower ribbon.

Trim stems of small fabric flowers. Pin in place on the ribbon at regular intervals around the hat.

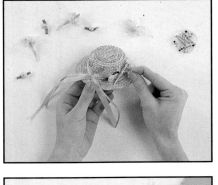

Sew flowers in place using double thread. Finish with a butterfly at the front. Center bonnet on card and attach by sewing through brim of hat and knotting threads on inside of card. A dab of glue will make knots secure. Arrange ribbons prettily.

A fun-for-Halloween card, quickly and easily made from paper and sequins. Cut red card 8½ by 6¼ inches (22 by 16cm). Score and fold 4¼ inches (11cm). Trace templates 39 and 40 on page 250 and make your own templates. Cut out a witch's hat from black paper. Cut the pumpkin head from orange paper or card, then cut out the eyes and mouth.

Position head and hat on card and mark with a sharp pencil. Glue pieces in place.

Use a store-bought 3–fold card with an oval, egg-shaped window. Place double-sided tape around the window and edges of the inside of the card. Peel off backing and attach strip of gold lace to bottom of oval. Cut a piece of satin slightly large than aperture. Stick down so that the satin side will show through window.

Add sequin stars and moons using rubber-based glue, holding them in place for a moment while the glue dries. Tweezers make handling the sequins easier.

Glue a large, jewel-like bead in the center of the "egg." Arrange beads, sequin leaves, and petals, then glue in position. Tweezers will make it easier to place them accurately.

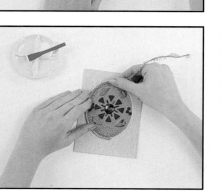

Finish with a smear of rubber-based glue around the edge of the egg on the outside of the card. Leave for a moment to become tacky, then press down some gold braid. Neatly trim the end of the braid.

The flowers used here are Victorian scrap or motifs. You could also cut flowers from magazines or old birthday cards. Cut card 10 by 7½ inches (25 by 19cm). Score and fold 5 inches (12.5cm) for top of card. Trace template 42 from page 250. Place tracing over gold card and draw again, using a sharp pencil which will indent the soft gold card.

A lace sachet of potpourri could be detached and used later to perfume a drawer. Potpourri can be bought in a variety of colors and perfumes. Cut card 9 by 7 inches (23 by 18cm). Score and fold 4½ inches (11.5cm). Cut out two lace flowers. Pin together and oversew leaving a gap to fill with potpourri.

Measure a border around edges of card and mark in pencil. Go over the border again in gold pen.

Make a funnel from a piece of paper and fill a lace sachet with potpourri. Oversew to close. Make a bow from narrow satin ribbon and curl ends over scissors.

Glue the cornucopia onto the card, then the flowers and fruit tumbling out. Add a white dove.

Cut three tissue paper leaves and glue onto the card. Sew bow onto sachet. Using a point of dividers or a thick sharp needle, make two holes at either side of the card, for positioning the sachet. Sew through and knot on back, securing with a dab of glue.

Cut card 8½ by 7½ inches (22 by 19cm). Score and fold 4¼ inches (11cm) for top. Into a plastic tray put two pints of cold water, mixed with ½ ounces (14g) of wallpaper paste. Leave for 15 minutes. In a small jar mix 1 inch (2.5cm) of oil paint from a tube and a little turpentine substitute. Apply drops of the mixed paint onto the surface of the water. Disperse with a wooden pick.

Place a piece of paper larger than the card gently on top of the water. Remove again fairly quickly, as soon as the paint has taken to the surface of the paper. Leave to dry on a sheet of newspaper. Press flat, if necessary, when dry. Cut to fit card and glue down.

Trace out a car from a magazine or postcard and transfer to glossy white paper. Cut out and glue down. Trace "chrome" details onto silver paper or card. Cut out and glue in place. Add details with silver pen.

Cut card 9 by 7 inches (23 by 18cm). Score and fold (4½ inches (11.5cm)). This is a spontaneous arrangement, so no two cards will look the same. Lay out a selection of blue materials: ribbon, sequin waste, buttons, feathers, and also tissue and silver paper. Tear tissue paper and cut chosen papers into random shapes. When you overlay strips of tissue, more shades of blue will occur.

Spray glue your materials and place in your favorite arrangement. Trim any excess. Tie a bow of narrow satin ribbon onto the base of the feather and trim ends diagonally. Attach to the card by sewing through.

To attach the duck button, make two holes with a sharp needle or the point of dividers, checking which way the button shank lies. Sew on the duck button from the back using double thread. Finish with a knot and secure with a dab of glue.

Cut gray marble-effect card 11 by 7½ inches (28 by 19cm). Score and fold 5½ inches (14cm). Trace out template 43 on page 250. Cut a piece of silver card to fit. Turn over and hold down with masking tape. Place tracing over card and attach with masking tape. Trace through onto card with a sharp pencil. Trace base onto a piece of black card.

With a sharp craft knife, cut out cup and base. Burnish edges of silver card by rubbing gently with the back of your thumbnail.

The tiny Bible is from a doll accessories' supplier. Cut card 9 by 8½ inches (23 by 22cm). Score and fold 4¼ inches (11cm). Trace cross template 41 on page 250 and transfer onto thin card to make your own template. Trace out onto gold paper and cut straight edges with a craft knife and ruler. The curved ends can be cut with scissors.

Glue the cup onto the card with spray glue. Draw in details with a sharp hard pencil. Finally, glue on base.

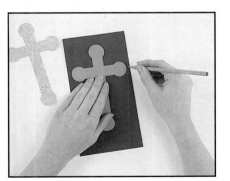

Lay the template on the card to position cross and mark with pencil. Spray glue on wrong side of the cross and attach to the card.

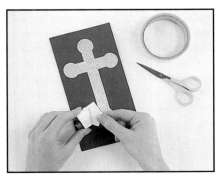

Stick a piece of double-sided tape on the back of the Bible. Peel off backing and attach to the cross at an angle.

Cut a circle of card 1¼ inches (3cm) in radius. Take approximately 38 inches (100cm) of single-sided 1 inch (2.5cm) wide pink satin ribbon. Pleat and machine sew round edge of card circle. Machine an inner circle of pleated blue ribbon. A wide zigzag stitch will hold pleats in place. Fold ends under to finish. Keep excess lengths of ribbon.

Cut green card 8½ by 6 inches (22 by 15cm). Score and fold 4½ inches (11cm). Cut a piece of traditional ledger-look marbled paper 6 by 3½ inches (15 by 9cm). Cut away top and bottom right-hand corners by measuring 1½ inches (4cm) along top and right-hand edges and bottom and right-hand edges.

Cut a circle of pink metallic paper or card ⅞ inch (2.2cm) in radius. Using leftover ribbon, cut two tails, one from each color and one longer than the other. Cut an inverted "V" shape at ends.

Spray glue on the back of the paper and attach to card so that there is a ¾ inch (2cm) margin of green card on the left-hand side. Punch a hole in the center along the right-hand edge of the front of the card.

Cut metallic card 9 by 7 inches (23 by 18cm). Score and fold 4½ inches (11.5cm). Glue tails in place over ends of pleated ribbon. Glue circle of pink paper or card in center of rosette. Attach rosette to card with glue.

Thread a length of brown satin ribbon through the hole and tie into a bow.

Purchase a 3–fold window card in a pale color, whichever size you prefer. Mark inner left-hand portion of card with a cross. Select an attractive picture, or focus on a detail from a magazine and lay a window over the picture. Mark four edges and corners with pencil dots.

Cut out picture slightly larger than the window. Place double-sided tape around the edges of the window inside the card. Stick down the picture using pencil guide marks to position. Fold over and stick down left-hand portion of card using double-sided tape.

The cats are purchased from a bead shop and attached to card with rubber-based glue. Hold in place for a minute or two until glue dries.

Make your own template from the dove 46 on page 250 and cut an extra template for the wing alone (see finished card). Draw round the dove twice on dark blue felt so that the birds face opposite directions and cut out. Cut two pieces of muslin 7 by 4½ inches (18 by 11.5cm). Position doves between two layers and pin. Baste layers together to hold doves in place.

Using two strands of embroidery thread, sew tiny running stitches around doves and stitch feet (see finished card). Place wing template over doves and lightly draw round with a sharp pencil. Quilt along these lines. When finished, take out basting thread and lightly press.

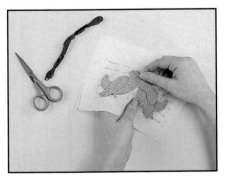

Purchase a 3–fold window card to fit quilted doves. Cut out a matching window from the left-hand section of card (see page 210). Trim muslin to about ¼ inch (6mm) larger than the window. Stick down using double-sided tape. Add tiny round bead for the doves' eyes and pearl beads to the corner of window.

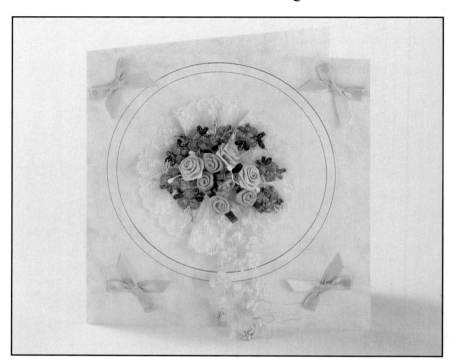

Cut card 8½ by 6¼ inches (22 by 16cm). Score and fold 4¼ inches (11cm). Trace template 48 on page 250 and transfer to thin card adding 4 inches (10cm) to depth, to match the card. Cut out and place on folded card. Draw round the church window shape at the top of the card and cut through both thicknesses. Draw a border with felt-tip pen.

Place several layers of different shades of pink tissue paper together in a pile on a cutting board. Cut round template 38 (page 250) to make approximately 10 hearts.

Spray glue the hearts and position on the card so that they overlap. You could stick more hearts inside the card and also leave some loose so that they scatter when card is opened.

Colors can be matched to those of the bridesmaid's dresses. Cut card 6 by 12 inches (15 by 30cm). Score and fold 6 inches (15cm). Bind a turquoise felt-tip pen to a compass and draw a double circle on the center of the card. Sew a line of running stitches along the edge of a strip of lace 18 inches (50cm) in length. Gather into a circle and sew the seam.

Sew ribbon flowers onto the center of a lace circle. Cut a strip of flower braid into single flowers and sew around ribbon flowers.

Sew on a couple of strings of ribbon flowers or braid to hang from the bouquet. Using a sharp needle or compass point, make several holes in card and sew on the lace bouquet from the back of the card using double thread. Tie a knot and add a dab of glue to secure. Glue on satin bows in four corners.

# POP-UP WEDDING CAKE

Cut card 12 by 6 inches (30 by 15cm). Score and fold 6 inches (15cm). Trace template 47 (page 250) and transfer to piece of white card. Cut a piece of white card 1 by 3½ inches (2.5 by 9cm) and score across ½ inch (1.25cm), 1 inch (2.5cm), 1½ inches (4cm) and ½ inch (1.25cm) for the stand. Decorate cake using felt-tip and silver pens before cutting out.

Glue down doily tablecloth on the base of the card. In pencil, draw two lines 1 inch (2.5cm) either side of the fold in the center. This is your guide for placing cake stand. Glue a 1½ inch (4cm) section to the back of the cake. Then place bottom ½ inch (1.25cm) section on guideline and glue. Glue silver bows, bells, and horseshoes in place.

Glue the final ½ inch (1.25cm) section of the stand to the back of the card and hold until glue dries. Cut some tissue-paper confetti in colors to match the cake. Glue some to the tablecloth and leave some loose. Punch holes in four corners of the card. Thread curled silver ribbon through to tie and close card.

# GET WELL DAFFODILS

Cut card 8½ inches (22cm) square. Score and fold 4½ inches (11cm). Cut out a window 3½ by 6½ inches (9 by 16.5cm). Trace daffodils from a catalog or book and transfer onto cartridge paper. Paint with transfer paints. When dry, place over a square of polyester or polycotton fabric and press with a hot dry iron for 2 minutes. Carefully lift off paper.

Place print in an embroidery frame and pull until taut. To machine embroider, use same thread on top and bobbin. Take off présser foot and drop "feed dog" so that teeth will not hold work and you will be able to move it freely. Place embroidery ring under needle and drop pressure lever.

Moving machine wheel by hand, draw up bobbin thread to top and hold to start. Move ring, keeping your fingers on the edge of the frame and slowly "paint" with your needle. Experiment with stitches – length 0 and zigzag are good. Sew outline first, then color in. Press on reverse. Mount with double-sided tape and back with white paper.

Cut card 18 by 8 inches (45 by 20cm). Score and fold at 6 inches (15cm) and 12 inches (30cm) to form 3–fold. Follow chart on page 251. You may vary the yarns and use up odds and ends. Most yarn is used double on 12 holes to 1 inch (2.5cm) canvas. Find the center point of the canvas and draw on the fireplace design with felt-tip pens.

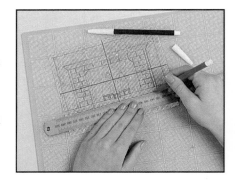

Start in the center, working the fire in random long stitch and tent stitch, varying the colors of the flames. Next, work the fire basket in tent stitch.

Cut card 8½ by 6 inches (22 by 15cm). Score and fold 4¼ inches (11cm). Trace templates 44 and 45 (page 250). Transfer onto green card for the bedhead, and brown for bunny's head. Cut them out, plus an oblong of white paper for a pillow. Trim edges of pillow with pinking shears.

Continue with the copper fireguard in slanting satin stitch, fire surround in tent stitch, brickwork in long stitch, carpet in tent stitch, and walls in long stitch. For the rug, lay a wooden pick across the canvas and work stitches over the pick. Cut loops to make the pile. When finished, trim and cut a window in the 3–fold card to fit the piece. Mount with double-sided tape.

On good quality drawing paper, draw a patchwork quilt. Fill in squares with transfer paint following the manufacturer's directions. Iron the painting onto a piece of bonded facing or synthetic fabric. Trim to fit bed.

Spray glue the backs of all pieces and attach to card in order: bedhead, pillow, bunny, and quilt. Draw in bunny's features with a fine felt-tip pen. Add wallpaper pattern using groups of four dots to look like flowers.

Trace template 52 (page 251). Transfer outer balloon onto blue card, inner balloon onto white card, and also onto the tracing paper side of fusible web. Number each segment and cut out. Mark on the blue balloon where the inner balloon will fit. Iron balloon segments onto the wrong side of three fabrics. Cut out carefully and peel off backing.

Place balloon segments onto the white card balloon and press with a dry iron. Trim edges and using the guide on the main blue balloon, glue down. Cut a small piece of fabric for the basket with pinking shears and glue in place.

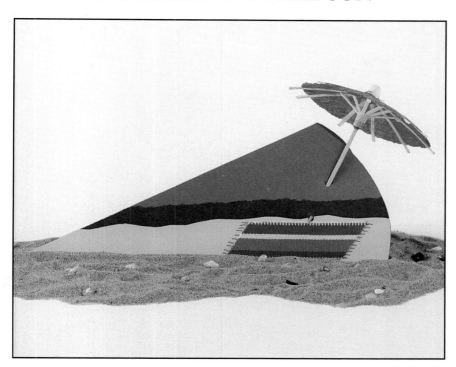

Idyllic lazy days, beachcombing in yellow sand under blue sky. Trace template 51 (page 251) and transfer to blue card. Score down the center.

Draw in ropes, then the basket design on fabric using a brown felt-tip pen. Score the base of balloon where indicated on the right side and fold back so that the balloon will stand. If being mailed, this card should have an extra piece of card in the envelope for protection.

Tear blue tissue paper to resemble the sea. Cut a piece of yellow paper with a curved top edge to make it appear that the waves are breaking. Place the pieces wrong side up in a spray booth and spray glue. Fix to the card and trim to fit.

Cut a piece of striped fabric or paper to make a beachtowel. Draw fringe on the towel with a felt-tip pen. Glue in place. Punch two holes and insert a beach umbrella.

On good quality drawing paper, draw a 4¾ inches (12cm) square. Using a postcard or photograph as a guide, roughly draw in mountains, lakes, and grass. Color in with transfer paint, applied sparingly. The colors will not be true to the end product since they will change according to the fiber content of the material on which you print.

When paint is dry, place the paper over polycotton and press for 2 minutes with a hot dry iron. Try not to move the paper. You can make several prints from one painting. Mount the picture in an embroidery ring as shown. Follow your sewing machine's directions for free machine embroidery. Using a selection of threads, fill in areas using satin stitch and straight stitch.

Tie ends of satin stitch on the back when finished and press. Cut card 5½ by 11 inches (14 by 28cm). Cut a window 4½ inches (11.5cm) square. Attach the finished picture behind window using double-sided tape, then cut a piece of white backing paper and attach to the back of your work. Trim excess paper.

Cut card 8½ by 6 inches (22 by 15cm), score and fold 4¼ inches (11cm). Draw a border around the card, first in pencil, then in pink felt-tip pen. Roll out a piece of white modeling material until thin and cut a kite shape. Cut edges again with pinking shears.

Roll out lots of tiny pink balls for flowers and some long green sausages to be cut for stems. Roll out some flat lengths of pink clay to make a bow.

Fashion a giftwrap paper shape from the "kite" and place on a piece of aluminum foil. Slip green stems inside and press on flower balls with a wooden pick. Make a bow by folding pink lengths and shaping. Lay on foil and bake for 15–20 minutes at 275°F to harden. Leave to cool. Glue to the card and attach the bow.

A n unusual way to mark a 21st birthday and the traditional receipt of the key of the door. Cut a 8½ inch (22cm) square of bright silver card and score a fold down the center. Collect together some interesting shaped keys. Using a spray booth, place the folded silver card inside and lay the keys on the card in a pleasing arrangement.

Stenciling is a good way of making several cards quickly. Here gold spray paint was used. Stencil card is firm and flat so the paint does not spread under the edges. Cut a piece of stencil card large enough to cover cards. Using templates 49 and 50 (page 251), cut out stars with a sharp knife and ruler.

This cosmonaut was drawn by a six-year-old boy. Draw several rectangles 3½ by 5½ inches (9 by 14cm) and ask a child to draw some pictures. Photocopy it several times. The child will have great fun coloring in these drawings, perhaps each one in different colors. Cut card mounts to fit and stick down the drawings.

Use spray car paint, holding the can 8–10 inches (20–25cm) away from the card, and spray in a few short bursts to cover the whole card. Leave the first coat to dry for a few minutes and then spray a second coat. To ensure even distribution, you should carefully turn the card between coats. You may wish to spray a third coat. Use in a well-ventilated room.

When completely dry, remove the keys. You will not be able to get the cellulose paint off the keys easily, so be sure to use keys you no longer need. Other objects, such as old clock and watch parts, can also be used to make theme cards.

Shake a can of paint for a minute or two, then spray from a distance of 12 inches (30cm). A couple of coats gives a deeper color and the paint dries quickly. The stars you have cut from the stencil can also be used to make reverse image cards.

Gossamer-fine Japanese paper napkins make quick cards. Simply cut out designs and glue them to cards. With a sharp craft knife, cut a fan shape from a circular peacock napkin, so that the two large "eyes" are at top. Spray glue the back of the fan. Position and smooth onto a card.

Cut two more eyes from the napkin. Arrange, then spray glue on the wrong side and smooth down onto the card.

Experiment with different designs and cards to highlight the subtle colors. Butterflies on gold make an exotic card.

This magical, ever-rolling landscape is all in the imagination. It is made from layers of torn tissue paper and plastic iridescent. Cut pieces of card 6¼ by 10 inches (16 by 25cm). Score and fold 5 inches (12.5cm). Roughly tear several strips of tissue paper and cut iridescent film.

Arrange them on a sheet of 8 by 12 inch (21 by 30cm) paper so that the colors overlap and shade. When you are happy with your arrangement, turn the strips over and spray glue. You will find one side of tissue paper has more shine than the other. If there are gaps, you could fill them in with silver pen.

Divide a sheet of paper into six or more pieces and cut with a sharp craft knife. Each landscape can now be positioned on a card and glued.

W onderful abstract patterns can be produced by sprinkling salt on freshly painted silk. Cut a piece of fine white silk lining and place in an embroidery frame, pulling taut. Select the colors of silk paints you wish to use. Shake and carefully open the jars. Wet brush, then apply paint fairly swiftly and immediately sprinkle on salt. Fill frame with designs.

P otato cuts make quick but "impressionistic" prints. Choose a medium-size potato to fit comfortably into your hand. Cut in half and lay on it a motif cut from a piece of paper. Cut along the edge of the image, then slice the potato away all round the shape so that the image is raised. Dry on a paper towel.

Leave to dry, then brush off the salt. The silk will yield a variety of effects, so place different ready-cut window cards over the most attractive patterns. Mark the area to be framed in a window, then cut it out slightly larger. The smaller the window, the more designs you can make. You could also add embroidery, beads, and sequins to your designs.

A water-based, poster, or even fabric paint can be used. Apply paint to the potato image. Turn over and press gently but firmly onto card. Clean off paint with a tissue when you want to change color. Continue, making sure overlapping colors are dry.

Mount silk in the center window of a 3–fold card, using double-sided tape. Stick down the left-hand portion of card over the back of the silk.

Some cards will be better than others, but this is part of their charm. Finish off a candle card with gold pen flame and "surround.".

Beautiful giftwrap lasts a little longer made into a quick and effective card. Cut card, then score and fold. Cut giftwrap a little larger. Glue the wrong side of the giftwrap and lay it flat. Position the first half of the card on paper and smooth. Bring up giftwrap to adhere to the other half of card, but leave room for fold. Smooth down.

Trim edges with a sharp knife. Affix ribbon on four sides on the inside of the card with a little piece of double-sided tape. Tie ribbon in a bow.

Carefully transfer to aluminum foil with a spatula or knife. Bake the cake according to the manufacturer's directions. The cake may stretch, but you can trim it with scissors after baking. Glue doily tablecloth on card. Cut spotted ribbon and fold around the bottom of the cake. Attach with double-sided tape or glue and add second ribbon trim.

Cut pink glossy card 6 by 8½ inches (15 by 22cm), score and fold 4¼ inches (11cm). Draw out cake shape onto thin card and cut out to make a template. Warm a ball of modeling material in your hands and roll out until thin. Place the template on clay and cut round with a knife. Make a little dent in the top center where the candle will fix.

Photographs of flowers can be mounted on cards and sent to friends during winter months. Make a collection over the summer. Make a mask of the right size so that you may frame the most effective image. Mark four corners with a compass or sharp pencil point. Cut off excess with ruler and craft knife. Spray glue to mount.

Wipe the back of the cake with lighter fuel to remove any grease. Dab rubber-based glue on the back of the cake and wait until tacky before fixing to the card. Spread a fine line of glue along the candle and apply to the card. Hold in place for a minute or two until the glue dries.

# TEMPLATES

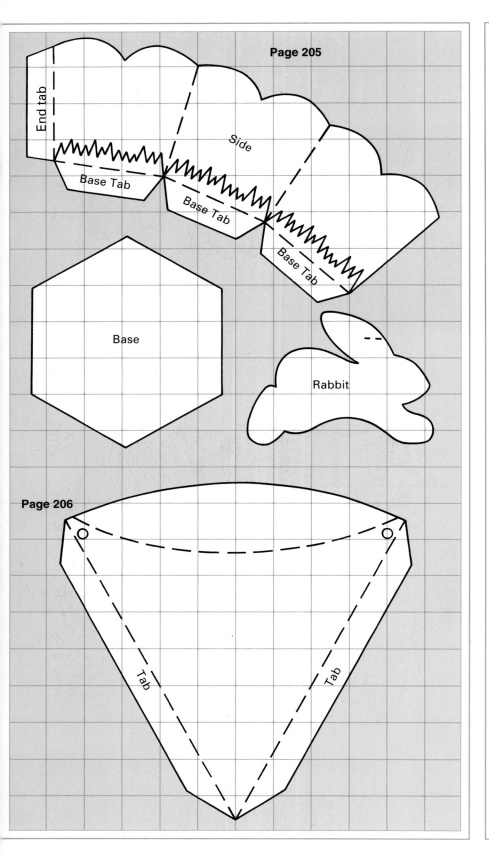

Page 205

End tab

Side

Base Tab

Base Tab

Base Tab

Base

Rabbit

Page 206

Tab

Tab

Page 211

Page 74

Page 211

Harvest storage jars (page 62)

Brilliant boxers (page 68)

Rosy Scarf (page 69)

Page 106:
Each square = 2cm (¾in)

Page 107: Each square = 2cm (¾in)

Page 110:
Each square = 2cm (¾in)

Page 110: Each square = 2cm (¾in)

Page 111: Each square = 2cm (¾in)

Page 94: Each square = 2.5cm (1in)

Page 94: Each square = 2.5cm (1in)

Page 126: Each square = 2.5cm (1in)

Page 126: Cut same size

**Page 187**

**Page 187**

**Page 36:**
Each square = 1.5cm (⅝in)

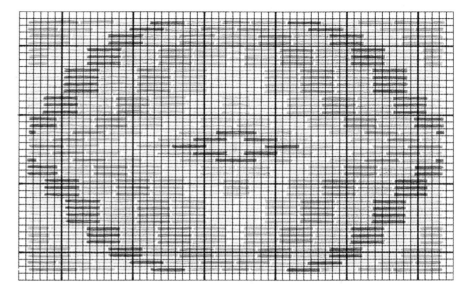

Needlepoint in Lilac (page 216)

A Warm New Home Welcome (page 236)

The following are designs for the various boxes described in this book. Draw the templates out carefully, following either the imperial or the metric measurements – do not use a combination of both. To score the fold lines, run along the dotted lines – on the inside of the box – with the back of a craft knife or the blunt edge of a pair of scissors; this will help you to fold the box more easily. If you wish to increase or decrease the size of your box, just scale the measurements up or down as required.

## Squared Up (page 162)

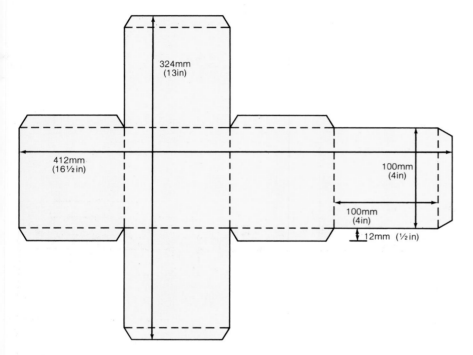

324mm (13in)

412mm (16½in)

100mm (4in)

100mm (4in)

12mm (½in)

## Box Clever (page 162)

12mm (½in)

New flap

New box top

Match to side measurement

25mm (1in)

New flap

New flap

New flap

Measure side of ceral packet

100mm (4in)

Existing flap

Existing flap

Existing flap

Existing flap

Existing flap

## Diamonds Are Forever (page 163)

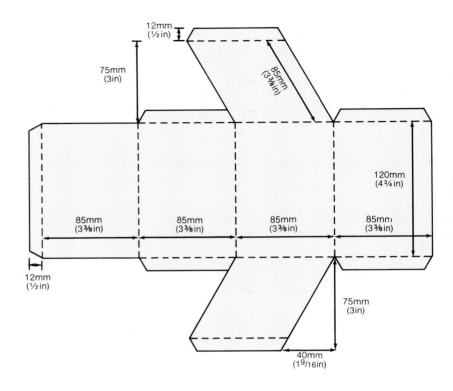

12mm (½in)

75mm (3in)

85mm (3⅜in)

120mm (4¾in)

85mm (3⅜in)

85mm (3⅜in)

85mm (3⅜in)

85mm (3⅜in)

12mm (½in)

75mm (3in)

40mm (1⁹⁄₁₆in)

## Floral Tribute (page 164)

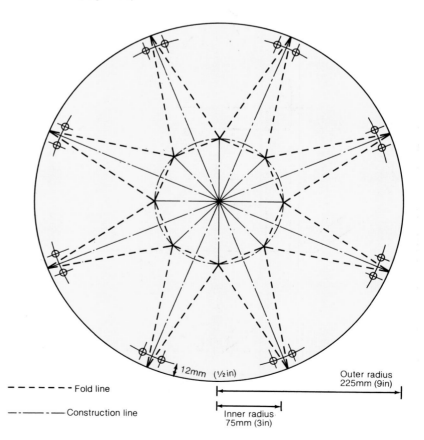

12mm (½in)

– – – – – Fold line

– · – · – · – Construction line

Outer radius 225mm (9in)

Inner radius 75mm (3in)

252

## Handle With Care (page 164)

18mm (3/8 in)
25mm (1 in)
Radii of handles

50mm (2in)
50mm (2in)
50mm (2in)
2mm (1/8 in)
100mm (4in)
100mm (4in)
100mm (4in)
100mm (4in)
100mm (4in)
200mm (8in)
100mm (4in)
200mm (8in)
12mm (1/2 in)

## The Pyramids (page 165)

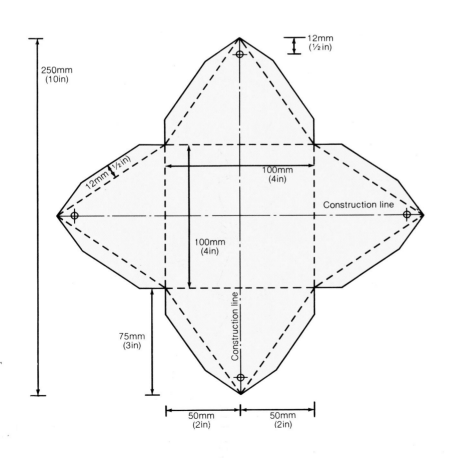

250mm (10in)
12mm (1/2 in)
100mm (4in)
12mm (1/2 in)
Construction line
100mm (4in)
Construction line
75mm (3in)
50mm (2in)
50mm (2in)

## Smart Sachets (page 166)

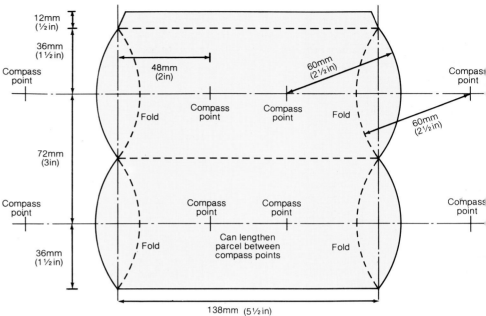

12mm (1/2 in)
36mm (1 1/2 in)
Compass point
48mm (2in)
60mm (2 1/2 in)
Compass point
Compass point
Compass point
Fold
Fold
60mm (2 1/2 in)
72mm (3in)
Compass point
Compass point
Compass point
Compass point
Fold
Can lengthen parcel between compass points
Fold
36mm (1 1/2 in)
138mm (5 1/2 in)

## Boxed In (page 167)

10mm (3/8 in)
44mm (1 3/4 in)
10mm (3/8 in)
10mm (3/8 in)
22mm (7/8 in)
5mm (3/16 in)
7mm (1/4 in)
15mm (5/8 in)
2mm (1/8 in)
30mm (1 1/4 in)
84mm (3 1/4 in)
30mm (1 1/4 in)
84mm (3 1/4 in)
84mm (3 1/4 in)
12mm (1/2 in)
30mm (1 1/4 in)
35mm (1 3/8 in)
15mm (1 3/8 in)

## Woven Hearts (page 195)

175mm (7in)
75mm (3in)
Cut slit
Cut slit
Compass point
Compass point